CHRISTIANITY AS PSYCHOLOGY

The Healing Power of the Christian Message

Morton Kelsey

AUGSBURG Publishing House • Minneapolis

CHRISTIANITY AS PSYCHOLOGY
The Healing Power of the Christian Message

Library of Congress Cataloging-in-Publication Data

Kelsey, Morton T.
  CHRISTIANITY AS PSYCHOLOGY.

  Bibliography: p.
  1. Christianity—Psychology. 2. Spiritual
healing. I. Title.
BR110.K375   1986   261.5'15   85-22864
ISBN 0-8066-2194-X

Manufactured in the U.S.A.   APH 10-1184

    3   4   5   6   7   8   9   0   1   2   3   4   5   6   7   8   9

To friends and colleagues
who are bridging the gap:
Jeanne Strano-Thomas, George Lough, Douglas Daher,
Timothy Kochems, John Vara, Royal Alsup,
James and Eileen Maronde.

Other Books by Morton Kelsey

God, Dreams, and Revelation:
A Christian Interpretation of Dreams

Encounter with God: *A Theology of Christian Experience*

Healing and Christianity

Myth, History and Faith: *The Remythologizing of Christianity*

The Christian and the Supernatural

The Other Side of Silence: *A Guide to Christian Meditation*

Can Christians Be Educated? *A Proposal
for Effective Communication of our Christian Religion*

The Cross: *Meditations on the Seven Last Words of Christ*

Discernment: *A Study in Ecstasy and Evil*

Dreams: A Way to Listen to God

Tales to Tell: *Legends of the Senecas*

The Age of Miracles: *Seven Journeys to Faith*

Afterlife: *The Other Side of Dying*

Adventure Inward: *Christian Growth
through Personal Journal Writing*

Reaching for the Real

Caring: *How Can We Love One Another?*

Transcend: *A Guide to the Spiritual Quest*

Tongue Speaking: *The History
and Meaning of Charismatic Experience*

Prophetic Ministry: *The Psychology
and Spirituality of Pastoral Care*

Christo-Psychology

Companions on the Inner Way: *The Art of Spiritual Guidance*

Resurrection: *Release from Oppression*

CONTENTS

PREFACE

For many years the relation of clinical psychology and Christianity has been one of my principal concerns. As a young minister in a thriving parish, I experienced emotional problems and confusions and the physical dysfunctioning that usually goes along with them. I looked around the church for someone who could untangle my mind-soul, my psyche, and I could find no one there who really knew much about the depth and complexity of the mind and how it related to the soul and who was at the same time a person I could trust. In a hierarchical institution like the church, few people wish all of their most intimate idiosyncracies passed on. Through my friend, Dorothy Phillips, I was led to Jungian analyst, Max Zeller. Within a few months my life was turned around by a man who knew the deepest meaning of anxiety, a Jew who had escaped Nazi Germany. Also, he knew the saving power of God and could help me listen to the voice of a healing God, who, I discovered, was seeking to help me come to wholeness and health. However, in my religious training as a child or as a seminary student, I had not been taught how to listen to that inner voice and understand the messages that were being given to me.

As I looked back over the experience of coming back to life, stability, and a new burst of creativity, I was puzzled. The method through which the turnaround had been accomplished recognized the depth and complexity of the human soul. I had been listened to without judgment by someone showing genuine caring about me and my family, having a vision of what wholeness meant and an understanding of the necessity of having me find my own particular meaning as part of a meaningful universe. Thus I was free to reveal all of myself. Max Zeller also showed me ways of relating to God, who alone could reveal to me where I got off the track and how I could get back on.

As I reflected, I realized that all of what I had experienced in the office of a secular psychologist-therapist was implicit in the full Christian message and story. I had experienced the wisdom and love that Jesus of Nazareth had taught and lived in his incarnation, in his outreaching healing love, and in his death and resurrection. Christian spiritual directors throughout the centuries had used these very methods of bringing suffering human beings to wholeness. When I visited with Carl Jung, he told me that his therapeutic practice was closer to that of the classical spiritual directors in 19th-century France than it was to the psychological therapies current at that time. Hilde Kirsch, with whom I worked for many years, once said to me: "You know, Morton, there is no reason that there can't be healing within the church as well as in the psychologist's office." I read a great deal of Jung and was intrigued by his often-repeated statement that the full Christian dogmatic system met every human psychological need. He also noted that among those who came to him for therapy, he found very few people who were firmly based within the full Christian message.

Over the years I have written on many aspects of Christian practice and their therapeutic effect upon those who use them. As I studied tongue speaking, I realized that both historically and in my own parish this recurring biblical phenomenon produced dramatic transformation in the lives of some of those who experienced it, and thus I wrote *Tongue Speaking*. It was through dreams that I had been first led to hear the Holy Spirit speaking to me. I reread the Bible and then the church Fathers and realized that both the Bible and the Fathers of the church saw the dream as one of the most common ways that God communicated to human beings; this study resulted in *God, Dreams, and Revelation*. Agnes Sanford introduced me to the healing ministry, and as I pored over the history of the church, I found that this ministry did not cease with the biblical narrative. I detailed the evidence for the importance of healing within the church in *Healing and Christianity*.

Through my Jewish Jungian mentor I also discovered that God still speaks to those who listen, just as he did to Samuel (1 Samuel 3). Again I realized nearly all Christian saints as well as most of the heroes and heroines of the Bible believed that the Divine Other wishes to communicate with human beings even more directly than through dreams. In *The Other Side of Silence* I showed, at the suggestion of Richard Payne, how Jungian psychology and Christian prayer deal with the same reality. When the director of book development at Augsburg Publishing House suggested that I explain how Christians might use a journal to facilitate their spiritual growth, *Adventure Inward* was written. In *Christo-Psychology* and *Prophetic Ministry* I have suggested ways in which Jung's thought and clinical practice can be used by Christians in pastoral care. And recently I wrote *Companions on the Inner Way*, reflections on the important and neglected practice of spiritual friendship, direction, or guidance, and how this relates to clinical psychology.

Some years ago Augsburg's book director asked me to write specifically about the psychological implications of Christianity and the Christian implications of psychology. Although I was much interested in the project, many other commitments were occupying my attention until I was asked to deliver the 1985 Finch Lectures at Fuller Seminary in Pasadena, California. I accepted the invitation and began to try to gather together the common themes that had been running through my life and writing for more than 20 years. During this period I reflected in depth on the central tenet of my faith, the resurrection of Jesus. I realized, probably for the first time, that Christianity is a cosmic drama of which the resurrection is the central act. However, the resurrection makes little sense except as it is seen in terms of God becoming incarnate in a broken and partially evil world, manifesting the nature of God as a human being and then, after the ascension and the giving of the Holy Spirit, asking us to respond to this divine drama of love.

Then I realized that the psychological implications of Christianity can be understood only as we refract the Christian mystery into its various magnificent colors through the prism of the biblical story. Jung and his followers had opened my eyes to the psychological implications of the Christian drama and had provided me with a world view in which the Christian message of transformation and salvation made sense. I also realized that both this world view and practice were supported from many other areas of modern thought.

Once these various insights came together, the pages that follow simply poured out. What is written here is what I perceive as the central Christian message and how it can transform our lives spiritually *and* psychologically. Spiritual transformation is much more likely to take place when we come to psychological wholeness—although this is not always the case. Jesus said: "I have come that they may have life, and have it to the full" (John 10:10). In the light of Jesus' healing ministry this statement undoubtedly refers to this life as well as our life in the world to come.

Many people have contributed to the insights that are presented here. Max Zeller, Hilde and James Kirsch—all Jungian analysts—introduced me to the practice of Jung and to the depth of his psychological and philosophical thought. A visit with Jung in Küssnacht confirmed his authenticity; he made no pretensions to being other than a medical doctor. The people of St. Luke's Church in Monrovia, California, encouraged me to pursue this way, helped me take a sabbatical at the Jung Institute in Zürich, and facilitated the formation of a psychological clinic at the church, where Jungian analysts and clergy trained in a Jungian framework ministered to people within the church as well as to people coming to us from all over the Southwest. Dr. Leo Froke, a psychiatrist in a neighboring town, and I met biweekly for lunch for many years to discuss the relation of religion, literature, and psychology; he introduced me to the wide field of modern therapeutic psychology.

In 1969 I was asked to teach in the Graduate Department of Education at the University of Notre Dame. An excellent counseling and guidance program was part of this department, and I learned much from many of the professors there, particularly C. William Tageson. Many of the students, graduate and undergraduate, came to me with problems of meaning that were not being dealt with in any official way in the university. Many of the students went on into clinical psychology and psychiatry, and through the years they have kept me in contact with the latest developments in their fields. In particular, these included Douglas Daher, Jeanne Strano-Thomas, John Vara, George Lough, Timothy Kochems, Royal Alsup, and James and Eileen Maronde. All the ideas presented here have been discussed many times with Andrew Canale, who has worked with the subject matter of this book for 10 years. It was Dr. Canale who suggested that an introduction of this nature was necessary for those not acquainted with my other writing.

In 1982 a program of Christian Spiritual Disciplines was inaugurated at San Francisco Theological Seminary with Dr. Roy Fairchild as professor of Spiritual Life and Psychology. It was made possible by the interest and generosity of Robert and Betty Buffum. I have worked closely with Dr. Fairchild and the seminary in implementing this program designed to deal with the issues presented here.

Some years ago Fuller Seminary started a graduate program in psychology at the suggestion of Dr. John Finch. The basic substance of this book was presented there as the annual integration lectures within that school. Dr. Finch was present and concurred with the essential thrust of the lectures. The respondents to these lectures, Hendrika Vande Kemp, C. Peter Wagner, and Russell P. Spittler suggested many additions to the original lectures; questions from the floor also clarified many issues. At Fuller Seminary there is indeed a growing awareness of the fact that open-minded clinical psychological practice and transforming Christian spiritual practices need to befriend one another.

For 30 years John Sanford and I have been close friends and have worked on the relationship of clinical psychology, religious experience, and Christianity. His many books and our frequent personal discussions have been invaluable for me in coming to the conclusions that I have reached in this area. My wife, Barbara, has also been involved in the study of psychology, sociology, and religion, and together we have explored, examined, and pondered how human beings can truly be whole and God-centered. My children, now mature adults, have taught me more about what human beings feel and how they react than anyone else. In their younger years they endured a father who spent great amounts of time listening to other people and writing. John Neary, a former student at Notre Dame and now professor of English, edited and clarified my prose, and Cindy Wesley turned an abominable typescript into a readable manuscript. Paisley Roach prepared the index and Rosalind Winkelholz secured permissions. To all of these people I am deeply grateful.

Gualala, California
Easter 1985

INTRODUCTION

Several years ago Paul Vitz wrote a critique of humanistic psychology entitled *Psychology as Religion: The Cult of Self-Worship* (Eerdmans, 1977). He presented an excellent case that many of the leading humanistic thinkers—Fromm, Rogers, Maslow, and Rollo May—were deifying the human personality, the human psyche. In this deification of the human being they were proposing not only inadequate psychology, but a very inferior brand of religion. In the pages that follow I will make the opposite suggestion about Christianity. When the full divine drama of Christian faith is understood, accepted, and fully lived, we find not only the most adequate religious expression available to humankind but also a profound psychological understanding and method. This psychology can integrate all that secular psychology has to offer and can in addition deal with a host of the emotional problems caused by the meaninglessness and the low-grade depression that are so much a part of our Western culture. I will argue, in other words, that the full message of Christianity has always offered the hope not merely of salvation in a world to come but of healing and wholeness *in this world.*

In order to support this thesis I will briefly examine the healing emphasis in the Christian tradition, as well as the present-day misery and lostness that prod human beings to seek psychological help. We shall then look at the major schools of psychological thought and see how different they are in their ideas about human beings and the ways to treat them. Next we shall assess each of these viewpoints and see which of them deals most adequately with the full gamut of human experience. We shall then describe the full Christian drama, which Jung called the finest and most complete therapeutic system ever given to human beings. And we shall continue with some suggestions about how we can step into the action of this divine drama and share in its healing, transforming power. How can we allow our conscious acceptance of Jesus of Nazareth to be integrated into the full depth of our entire human psyche? We shall conclude by pointing out the implications of Christian life, practice, and belief for psychologists and psychological practice.

1

No Room for God in Psychology and Healing

Jesus of Nazareth spent a major portion of his ministry healing the bodies, souls, and minds of those around him. And the vital early church continued Jesus' ministry of healing along with that of preaching and teaching. Many of the letters of Paul and others, as well as the Acts of the Apostles, describe a similar ministry, and this tradition has continued throughout the Christian church. This emphasis, in fact, never ceased within the Greek Orthodox tradition; in the Western church, however, this aspect of ministry suffered first from the inroads of the rationalism of Aristotle in scholasticism and then from the pervasive influence of the agnostic "Enlightenment" of the past two or three centuries.

In the West, secular thinking has engulfed society and even the church, and this secularism taints every one of us brought up in the Western world. From this secular point of view God, religion, faith, and the resurrection of Jesus have little or nothing to do with psychology or psychiatry, or with the healing of any sort of human misery. Religion was left with only a shadowy soul-spirit, and secular thought even cast doubt on the existence of that.

The questions naturally arise: Does God have a place in psychological healing, in psychotherapy, in the formation of the mature, optimal personality? Is religious faith in the risen Christ an aspect of reality that needs to be taken into consideration by those who would help us through our psychological dis-ease to wholeness and meaning? Should psychologists take into consideration the religious development of their patients as part of their data? Is experience of God or the resurrected Jesus or the Holy Spirit a genuine experience of reality? Does this experience have a positive or negative effect on our psychological development and healing?

When I am asked about the relation of religion and psychology, I usually answer with two staccato questions: Which psychology? Which religion? Psychology has three quite different branches. First there is *psychobiology*, which is interested in studying the brain and the glandular system to understand the relationship of human experience to the physical mechanism of the body. Then there is *experimental psychology*, which is interested in studying how human beings react, how they function, and how they perceive, understand, think, suffer, and learn. Last of all there is *clinical psychology*, which is dedicated to treating suffering and psychologically disabled people in order to relieve their suffering and enable them to function as adequately as possible. Carl Jung once commented on the difference between *experimental psychology*, which views itself as an exact science, and *clinical psychology*, which is a healing profession: "In experimental psychology the experimenter asks the questions and the subject answers. In clinical psychology the suffering patient asks the questions, and the therapist tries to answer. Guess which one asks the more difficult questions?"

Psychobiology and experimental psychology are certainly legitimate and worthwhile areas of study, but both of them consider the question of meaning and value to be out of their province, and the matter of God is utterly irrelevant to them because they limit themselves to considering the data of the five senses. Meaning and religious experience are difficult, if not impossible, to discuss if we are limited to the data of verifiable sense experience.

Even within clinical or healing psychology, with which we shall be primarily concerned in the pages that follow, there are five quite different psychological traditions that offer very dissimilar answers to questions about the relevance of religion to clinical practice. These varied psychological viewpoints are based on different ideas about the universe and the human person, as well as on widely differing psychological data. For example, some psychological schools view religion as a retreat into an infantile dependency; others, as a necessary element in coming to human maturity. There are, in short, almost as many contradictory ideas about human maturity to be found among psychologists as there are Protestant denominations.

Before we take a look at these contrasting views and then try to decide which of them is most adequate, let us look at the reasons people come to psychologists and counselors.

In 1980 the American Psychiatric Association, the World Health Organization, the National Institute of Mental Health, and several other groups working in mental health prepared a new description of the categories of mental disorders called *Diagnostic and Statistical Manual III*. Dr. Gerald May has described these categories well in his book, *Care of Mind/Care of Spirit: Psychiatric Dimensions of Spiritual Direction* (Harper & Row, 1982). First of all, May says, there are *organic difficulties*—inadequate brain structures or portions of the brain damaged by disease or tumor. Closely related are *substance-use disorders;* drugs can impair or distort brain activity and functioning, and alcoholism has been called "self-induced psychosis." Then there are individuals who do not seem to be in touch with the common reality that the rest of us take for granted; we call such people *psychotic*. Their inner world is more real to them than the outer one, and they actually mistake their inner reality for outer reality. They may have simple delusions (believing they are Napoleon or Jesus Christ) or irrational swings of mood, or they may think that people are persecuting them or that their bedrooms are bugged. And then there is the vast array of problems which used to be called *neuroses* but which now are classified in a variety of ways; for our purposes, however, we can retain the word *neurotic* to signify the problems that do not fall in those first three categories. People suffering from *neurotic* afflictions are not able to manage their lives as they would like to. None of these problems are rarities; in a study released in October 1984, the National Institute of Mental Health found that 19% of the American population over 18 years of age suffer from at least one psychiatric disorder during any six-month period.[1]

Of those people who come to psychologists or psychiatrists for help, most come for one or several of the following reasons.

1. They are beset with irrational fears and anxieties (*phobias*).

2. They find themselves doing things that they don't want to do; they have *compulsions*.

3. They are unable to do the things that they want to do; they have inner roadblocks that need to be removed.

4. They are depressed, even though life is going well; life has lost its luster and value for no apparent reason. The number of words in English for this condition indicates the enormous dimensions of this problem, as do the statistics on the prevalence of depression.

5. Many people find that they have lost their meaning, and there is no reason to go on and even try to function.

6. Some people have altered states of consciousness or experiences that do not fit the norm, and they don't know how to deal with them.

7. Some people have inner experiences in which they seem to be torn apart, struggling against evil, destructive forces that seem to be trying to destroy them.

8. More and more people come to psychological counselors asking for spiritual guidance, having become aware of the spiritual dimensions of reality and knowing of nowhere else to turn. The lack of such facilities in our churches is a Christian scandal.

9. There are many people who seek psychological help because their psychological problems are creating unpleasant or even dangerous physical symptoms. Psychosomatic medicine developed out of the work of psychologists who realized that emotional turmoil can cause physical illness.

10. Many people are brought to professional counselors because they have broken the law or because relatives are concerned about their strange behavior.

I am quite sure that a large amount of this distress and psychological illness is the result of being cut off from meaning and God, of lacking any vital religious life. Western culture has created a religious vacuum, and meaninglessness is a serious sickness.

Agnes Sanford used to describe the difference between *psychotic* problems and *neurotic* ones in a humorous and simple way. According to Sanford, the neurotic says, "Two and two are four, and I can't stand it." The psychotic exclaims, "Two and two are twenty-two; isn't it wonderful!" "The neurotic builds castles in the air and complains bitterly that they are inaccessible," Sanford said. "The psychotic lives in them, and the psychologist collects the rent!"

In any case, the most adequate psychological framework will be the one that can deal with the full gamut of human misery. The best psychiatrist or psychologist is the one who knows brain chemistry, the effects of physical disease, the effects of an environment on human beings and their mental health, as well as the effects of the experience of God on human wholeness. This helping professional will also seek others knowledgeable in religious matters to whom to refer people with religious concerns. God is at least as observable as quarks are—probably much more so. The best religious psychological counselor or spiritual guide is the one who knows the full effect of living in a meaningless world or with misshapened religious ideas, and at the same time has enough medical knowledge to know when organic problems could be causing a particular condition. This guide will have available for referral medical and psychological experts when the individual exhibits symptoms beyond the spiritual director's competence.

There are many different ways of classifying the welter of psychological theories and practices. My analysis is based on each theory's view of human nature and of the world in which we live.

1. There is first of all the medical-biological view that the human being is essentially a physical machine with defects that need to be fixed physically or chemically.

2. Closely allied to this is the behaviorist view that people are machines that can be programmed in the correct way or in an incorrect way; the psychologists are reprogrammers.

3. The humanist view states that human beings cannot be reduced to a physical mechanism, but that there is nothing transpersonal to aid us in bringing the human being to wholeness. According to humanists the task of the counselor is to free individuals to ascend to their natural human potentials.

4. Sigmund Freud—one of the founders of modern psychiatry, and a great genius—provided a fourth viewpoint. He believed that we human beings are conditioned by our psychic inheritance. For Freud the task of the therapist was to help

human beings strip away their illusions and face the ultimately meaningless, cold-war struggle that takes place among the id, the death wish, the conscience (the repressive superego), and our rational adult egos. Freud might be called a pessimistic transpersonal psychologist; he saw forces beyond consciousness, but he felt that they were destructive and primitive, and had to be withstood. In the Freudian schema, human beings fight alone against a meaningless world.

5. And lastly there are those psychologists who believe that there is a transcendent transpersonal realm and that humans fail to come to their full potential unless they are touched and transformed by it. According to such theorists, life continues after death, and we need to prepare for this future life. Human beings have an eternal destiny.

Medical-Biological and Behavioristic Theories of Healing

I wish to look more closely first at the medical-biological approach to human personality. Some representatives of this school write statements like this: "Divine explanations are not a basis for scientific understanding, just as scientific understanding does not nullify religious concepts."[2] Most of the thinkers in this school, however, take for granted that the mind and personality are more or less reducible to the brain and physical organism, and that talk about God or meaning is nonsense. The hardware of our physical organism is the result of a random mechanical evolutionary process, and human personality is little more than an expression of that mechanism.

Melvin Konner's *The Tangled Wing: Biological Constraints on the Human Spirit* (Holt, Rinehart, and Winston), published in 1982, is up-to-date and consistent. From Konner's point of view the human being, as a person and a mechanism, is merely the means through which the genes reproduce themselves. The author never looks seriously at the idea that human beings could have more significance than this or that there might be some divine meaning in the universe. A more popular presentation of this basic idea can be found in an article in the United Airlines' in-flight magazine for June 1983. There Tim Hackler proclaimed that depression is simply a matter of chemical imbalance in the brain, and since we now have the right chemicals we can dismiss the whole subject. For Hackler, the problem was completely solved. This point of view would be funny were it not so tragic.

There is no doubt that brain research and the study of the effects of the various hormones on mood and activity are important. Some of the breakthroughs in providing drugs are of enormous help in treating some kinds of mental and emotional distress, and these drugs should be known and used. However, such study in itself is a far cry from seeing human personality as merely a mechanism. Human distress, grief, fear, and meaninglessness can create a chemical imbalance just as easily as a chemical imbalance can create the emotional difficulties. Human beings need love, creativity, and inner harmony, as well as some meaningful experience of transcendence, if they are to maintain a proper chemical balance as living organisms. Dr. Candace Pert, one of the team of brain researchers responsible for the discovery of the endorphins, is a leading student of the brain. She perceives the brain as an instrument of meaning and purpose. There are others who take the same stance, but they are a small minority.[3]

Another group of theorists, the behaviorists from Watson to Skinner, operate from the same basic world view that underlies the medical-biological approach to human personality, but behaviorists have a very different method of dealing with human problems. The psychobiologists, as we have seen, identify the mind, personality, and consciousness with the physical organism. These thinkers consider talk about mental phenomena in any but physical terms to be superstitious babble about "the ghost in the machine." They maintain that the most effective way to change personality is through physically altering the machine with surgery, shock treatment, or chemicals, and that in the long run the only way to change human beings is through genetic engineering.

The behaviorists, though, start with the premise that the human being at birth is a blank sheet of paper. Our task, they claim, is to provide the best programming possible, and to change a human being's programming when it has not been adequate and has produced confused or mentally disturbed people. Behaviorists say that we learn our psychoses, our anxieties, and our depressions, and that these things can be unlearned as well.

We can be very grateful to psychobiologists for the great strides they have made in healing organic brain disease and for the chemical aids in dealing with psychoses and many neuroses without accepting the world view from which many of them operate. Likewise, behaviorism has taught us a great deal about the effects of positive reinforcement and has helped many people suffering from mental retardation and other specific problems.

Obviously these two schools are much opposed to each other, even though they operate from the same fundamental view of reality. From this shared point of view, the idea that God is creator and sustainer of the universe is as silly as the notion that human consciousness is a ghost running the machine. Like the psychobiologists, the behaviorists can study religious institutions and practices, but cannot deal seriously with what they profess. Although these two views differ theoretically, many health practitioners use the methods of both.

Again we must acknowledge the tremendous strides that have been made in learning theory and in how human beings respond to stimuli. Behaviorists have shown how much more effective rewards are than punishments in modifying behavior. While teaching at Notre Dame, however, I asked the students how they would determine whether to get help by going to the basically behavioristic psychology department or to the more humanistic counseling psychology available in the Department of Graduate Education. The students replied that you go to the psychology department if you have four legs and to counseling psychologists in the education department if you have two. They resented behaviorism's implication that they were to be manipulated by conditioning into a desired outcome. This idea, they felt, did not treat them as persons. Anthony Burgess' novel *A Clockwork Orange* (Norton, 1963), along with the film based on it, portrays the sinister aspect of such manipulative conditioning.

The essential problem with both the behavioristic and the medical-biological points of view is that, having limited themselves to observable, objectively verifiable data, they slip unconsciously into maintaining that these are the *only* data. This position rules out some very important human data: love, ecstasy, artistic inspiration, and religious experience. Gerald May wrote: ''In a purely psychiatric sense, any experience in which self image and sensory perceptions undergo a significant change in relationship within awareness could be called dissociative. Similarly the so-called altered states of awareness so often encountered in spiritual practice would generally be considered forms of dissociation.''[4] May is working within a framework that puts a great gulf between the religious and the psychiatric psychological point of view, although there seems to be no inherent reason why both of these viewpoints cannot be integrated into a single understanding of nature. If religious experience, however, is really based on a misperception of reality, and if the very idea of God is foreign to the categories of materialistic science, then there can in fact be no significant relationship between psychological healing and religion—and this is basically May's position.

Freud, the Great Innovator

Freud would have been quite happy if he could have accounted for all mental illness on the basis of physical causes, but he could not, and so he provided a theory very much at odds with these two materialistic ones. He did not deny that there are physical causes for mental illness, but he proposed that in addition to the brain and the conscious attitude, which he called the *ego,* there is in each of us a deep and hidden part of our personality that he called the *unconscious,* borrowing this term from popular thinking of his day. The nonphysical contents of the unconscious, such as wishes, fantasies, buried memories, and desires could result in painful physical and mental symptoms.

According to Freud, the ego enables us to manage our lives in relation to the outer world and other people. It also keeps us from being overwhelmed by our inner world. The unconscious contains our personal unconscious and also the pleasure-seeking principle, the *id,* which seeks sexual pleasure indiscriminately. An inner censor or *superego,* Freud claimed, keeps us from remembering the contents of the personal unconscious and from becoming aware of the id; we would find facing the desires of the id intolerable. Freud maintained that the censor even scrambles our dreams, which can reveal the real nature of the depth of ourselves. In his later years, Freud also came to believe that there is a *death wish* in each of us that is opposed to the life force of the id. The death wish seeks to drag us back into the deathlike immobility of inorganic reality. If we do not honestly face those horrors within ourselves and learn to deal with them, then we either fall into mental illness of one kind or another, and perhaps commit suicide, or we project them out onto other people. Such projections, according to Freud, are the source of human aggression and war.

Freud's thought can easily be diagramed. The two triangles pictured below represent the total human psyche, conscious and unconscious. The box represents the outer, material world with its physical limitations on the psyche. The small triangle stands for the ego, the center of consciousness that enables us to get around in the world. The unconscious is divided between the personal unconscious and the id. The censor stands between the total unconscious and the ego, protecting the ego from objectionable contents in the unconscious. The death wish is represented by the diagonal lines at the lower left of the id. Projections of the contents of the unconscious are represented by lines reaching out to other people, the other triangle. Although this theory does not explain all human behavior, it certainly has helped many people get a better handle on why they act as they do, and it has also enabled many to gain better control of their lives.

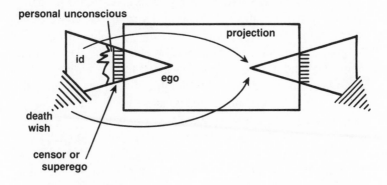

According to Freud, the conscious, disciplined human ego holding its rational own against the id, the death wish, the superego, and an often hostile world is the highest development in the universe. There is no religious help available from beyond the human ego. Indeed, in his book *The Future of an Illusion* (Norton, 1975), Freud describes religion as a regressive return to the womb, to dependence on something that does not exist. Religion was for him an avoidance of the cold, hard, bitter reality of life. For Freud, religious belief is detrimental to mental health, a reliance on illusion. In other words, Freud was very pessimistic about life, feeling that most of us are determined by subhuman forces. In a letter to Einstein he wrote that human beings will always go to war; if people don't project out the death wishes in aggression and war, Freud thought, they are likely to commit suicide.[5] In the light of this point of view we can admire even more Freud's courageous struggle against cancer during his last years.

The Third Force in Psychology

A reaction was bound to set in against these two deterministic branches of psychology, Freudian psychoanalysis and behaviorism (psychobiology has only been a significant contender in the last 30 years as we have learned more about the human brain and hormonal secretions that affect it). The humanists—psychologists well exemplified by Carl Rogers, Abraham Maslow, Erich Fromm, and Rollo May—believed that neither of these traditions did justice to the human being. In his recent book, *Humanistic Psychology: a Synthesis,* C. William Tageson wrote that the humanistic emphasis is "on this species-specific attribute: self-reflective awareness. . . . the notion of a *proactive* self, aware of its own existence, has certainly been a central, unifying characteristic of this movement."[6]

On the whole these thinkers are as optimistic as Freud was pessimistic. They see the goodness in human beings, and they believe that if people are treated with unconditional care, concern, and empathy, they will move toward self-actualization and wholeness. We human beings, these thinkers say, have an innate desire to grow and become caring and responsible people. But the most significant leaders of this movement have cut themselves off from any religious base. And, as Paul Vitz pointed out, without a God, the human psyche itself, from this point of view, tends to become the same as God. When we lack a God, we are likely to think of ourselves as God. In any case, though, the humanistic tradition has made a tremendous impact not only on the academic community but on the general public through the proliferation of self-help psychology books.

So much of what the humanists suggest about dealing with human beings has a Christian ring that it is necessary to listen very closely to them to hear that their faith is in *their own* love, not in God's love or in God's salvation; most of them never raise the possibility of being lifted up by God out of human lostness. Fromm, for example, writes that love for one's neighbor is not to be viewed as something transcending the human being. "It is something inherent and *radiating from* him. Love is not a higher power which descends upon man nor a duty which is imposed upon him; it is his own power by which he relates himself to the world and makes it truly his."[7] And in describing the qualities of the self-actualizing person, Maslow does not perceive belief in the divine as an essential quality of those whom he has selected as exemplifying it.

Rollo May, furthermore, wrote in his book *Existence* (Simon and Schuster, 1967): "I launch myself into the therapeutic relationship having a hypothesis, or *a faith, that my liking, my confidence, and my understanding of the other person's inner world,* will lead to a significant process of becoming" (italics added). And Carl Rogers declared in *On Becoming a Person* (Houghton Mifflin, 1961) that problems of the meaning of life and of helping people would always interest him, but he added, "I could not work in a field where I would be required to believe in some specified religious doctrine." Vitz stated that his experience teaching secular psychology at the university level suggested that "abandonment of one's 'religious background' is *reliably* assumed to be a rational consequence of getting an education, particularly in graduate schools." He went on to say that when God is thus dismissed and the problem of evil avoided, we have not only humanistic psychology, but humanistic religion taught in state-supported schools.

Still another school of thought valuing human consciousness and will is that of *cognitive therapy*. This viewpoint analyzes the bad thinking in which we have been trained and provides methods for consciously disengaging from these negative ideas and scripts.

We can learn much from the methods of humanistic psychology, in which human beings are really treated as human beings and related to with acceptance, empathy, and genuine caring. In a sense, the humanists are like the son in Jesus' parable who refused to go out into the field to work, and then went and did so. These psychologists, and particularly Carl Rogers, put into effect Jesus' radical idea of the value of every human being and the importance of unconditional love as the most important transforming power in the world. These humanists, in fact, often live Christianity far better than most Christians. In using their excellent interpersonal methods, however, we must not be beguiled into accepting their naive atheism or agnosticism.

According to Jesus, love is transforming because when we treat other people in this loving way we become channels of God's creative being. At St. Luke's Church in Monrovia, California, where I am rector emeritus, we learned the power of love in action through the teaching of Dr. Ollie Backus, who states again and again that we are not living Christianity until our lives express love toward one another, and that we cannot begin to love until we learn to listen to other people.

2

__ A Place for __ God in Psychology

In the last hundred years (and clinical psychology is only that old) there has been a growing realization that all of the therapies I have just described leave out something very important in their understanding and treatment of suffering human beings. In his Gifford Lectures in 1901–1902 (*Varieties of Religious Experience*), William James set the stage for this development. James described many examples of religious experience, often of the Christ, that brought people from miserable, ineffective agony to creativity and effectiveness. He wrote that the inability of many people to believe and be transformed by religious experience and faith "may in some cases be intellectual in its origin. Their religious faculties may be checked in their natural tendency to expand by beliefs about the world that are inhibitive, the pessimistic and materialistic beliefs, for example, within which so many good souls, who in former times would have freely indulged their religious propensities, find themselves nowadays, as it were, frozen; or the agnostic vetoes upon faith as something weak and shameful, under which so many of us today lie cowering, afraid to use our instincts.''[1] James' point is that beliefs about the world can have a profound effect on our psychological health.

Existential psychological thought was one reaction to the determinism of behaviorism and Freud. Some existentialists rejected most of Freud's thought, while others retained a large portion of it. Some of this school falls into the humanistic category above; Rollo May, Ludwig Biswanger, and Medard Boss are existential humanists. But other existential psychologists—including Karl Jaspers, Gabriel Marcel, Viktor Frankl, and John Finch—are specifically transpersonal. All existential psychologists urge an acceptance of freedom, a conscious acceptance of anxiety, and an openness to life's possibilities, but only members of the latter group find God an essential possibility to which we must be open if we are to come to our full human potential. Most of these writers, furthermore, place little emphasis on unconscious factors and influences.

Still other followers and associates of Freud accepted Freud's view of the dynamic unconscious, with its stress on the unconscious elements in the personality, but broke with his determinism, his pessimism, and his atheism. Roberto Assagioli, who founded an institute of psychosynthesis in Rome, wrote a book entitled *Psychosynthesis* (Penguin, 1976) in which he stated his belief that human beings cannot be whole unless they relate to the transpersonal spirit; Assagioli even provided methods to achieve this end. And in their later writings both Otto Rank and Alfred Adler came to many of the same conclusions, but the death of Rank at 52 and Adler at 62 kept them from developing this aspect of their thought.

It was Carl Jung who integrated a consideration of religion and religious experience into psychological thought more fully than any other psychologist. Jung lived to be almost 86 and wrote until three weeks before his death; during the final 15 years of his life—from the time of a nearly fatal illness and near-death experience until his death—Jung's main preoccupation was the significance of religious experience for psychiatry and psychology.

However, Jung's interest in religion and its importance in facilitating wholeness came to him much earlier as a result of his own inner struggle and experience. In 1932 Jung gave a talk to the Alsatian Pastoral Conference entitled "Psychotherapists or the Clergy." In it he said that for more than 30 years people had been coming to him from all the civilized countries of the world. "Among all my patients in the second half of life—that is to say, over thirty-five—there has not been one whose problem in the last resort was not that of finding a religious outlook on life. It is safe to say that every one of them fell ill because he had lost what the living religions of every age have given to their followers, and none of them has been really healed who did not regain his religious outlook."[2]

Jung also had an excellent philosophical background. He had read Kant's *Critique of Pure Reason* at age 18. He was well acquainted with the philosophical and scientific developments going on in the first part of the 20th century. Some of his patients and collaborators were those on the forefront of scientific thought, people like Wolfgang Pauli, Mircea Eliade, and Heinrich Zimmer. Leaders in many fields of thought met each year at Eranos at the home of a friend of Jung's in southern Switzerland to share their latest thinking. The papers presented there have been published. With the help of these great thinkers, Jung developed a carefully worked out philosophical framework in which God and the experience of God were integrated into a sophisticated world view and psychological theory.

This theory has clear and specific practical applications. For example, in *Let Go, Let God* (Augsburg, 1985), an excellent study of the spiritual significance of Alcoholics Anonymous, John Keller shows that before psychiatrists began to take seriously the spiritual dimension of alcoholism and addiction they were unable to bring healing to people with this affliction. He draws on the work of Dr. Harry Tiebout, a psychiatrist who worked with alcoholics. Keller, a Lutheran pastor who has spent more than 30 years in ministry with alcoholics, calls on the secular healing profession to look at the religious dimension in healing addiction and other mental illness. On the other hand, he asks the Christian community to hear the words of Dr. Albert Outler of Perkins School of Theology: the church, Outler has argued, will never have an adequate doctrine of the human person without the insights of psychiatry. Jung knew the founder of A.A. and wrote to him, calling alcoholism a "spiritual disease."

Dr. Roger Walsh, who earned a doctorate in psychology as well as a medical degree, wrote an article published in the June 1980 issue of the *American Journal of Psychiatry* entitled, "The Consciousness Disciplines and the Behavioral Sciences: Questions of Comparison and Assessment." In this careful, sophisticated statement, Dr. Walsh showed that much of modern psychiatry has ignored human experiences of the transpersonal. In doing so, he said, psychiatry has failed in its task of dealing with the *whole human being*. It is notable that in a television program on depression presented by the American Medical Association for credit for doctors on September 23, 1984, not one word was mentioned about lack of meaning or transpersonal experience in treating depression, the common cold of modern psychiatry. And yet depression is one affliction in which loss of ultimate meaning, lack of being in contact with God, certainly is a contributive factor.

Walsh quoted with approval a letter that Dr. Jung wrote to P.W. Martin in August 1945. Martin was a Quaker whose book, *Experiment in Depth* (Darby, 1982), was one of the first religious books to perceive the religious significance of Jung. "You are quite right," Jung wrote. "The main interest of my work is not concerned with the treatment of neuroses but rather with the approach to the numinous. But the fact is that the approach to the numinous is the real therapy and inasmuch as you attain to the numinous experiences you are released from the curse of pathology. Even the very disease takes on a numinous character."[3] Jung borrowed the word *numinous* from Rudolf Otto's *The Idea of the Holy;* the "numinous" is what human beings experience when in contact with God and the Holy. After Jung's break with Freud he was thrown into unconscious turmoil. He wrote that he survived because "I had an unswerving conviction that I was obeying a higher will." In later life Jung had a numinous near-death experience that he describes in a chapter entitled "Visions" in his autobiography, *Memories, Dreams, Reflections.*

Let us look at the philosophical and psychological framework that Jung proposed. Jung built on the work and ideas of those before and around him. He was knowledgeable in all areas of psychology and psychiatry, and he recognized the value of using a wide variety of techniques for healing patients. He saw the place for behavioral, cognitive, existential, and Freudian therapeutic methods, and he accepted the use of therapeutic drugs. He was critical of these methods only when they claimed to offer exhaustive accounts of the human psyche and when they neglected important data found in the religious search of humankind from the beginning of human consciousness.

A diagram may help us understand Jung's thought. As we compare this diagram with that representing Freud's view, we see that Jung changed the Freudian model in only four major ways; these changes, however, make a crucial difference. The triangle in the center presents one human being, and the whole diagram depicts the experiences that converge upon this individual. In a sense, the diagram depicts the entire universe

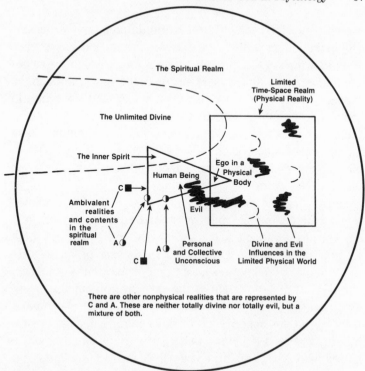

The Spiritual Realm

Limited
Time-Space Realm
(Physical Reality)

The Unlimited Divine

The Inner Spirit

Ego in a
Physical
Body

Human Being

Ambivalent
realities
and contents
in the
spiritual
realm

Evil

Personal
and Collective
Unconscious

Divine and Evil
Influences in the
Limited Physical World

There are other nonphysical realities that are represented by
C and A. These are neither totally divine nor totally evil, but a
mixture of both.

as one coherent whole. There is one unlimited spiritual domain under the direction of the unlimited divine. Jung usually referred to the spiritual realm as the *psychoid:* it is like the human psyche—conscious, knowing, willing, etc. (In his autobiography, *Memories, Dreams, Reflections,* and in his letters, Jung spoke directly about God, but in most of his other writings he used other terminology, hoping to reach the scientific communities.) Within and surrounded by the spiritual realm is the limited, physical, space-time, energy-mass world. Human beings in their essential nature are related to and embedded in both of these worlds. Through the five senses we receive knowledge of the physical dimension of reality; most of the data accepted by psychology and psychiatry is limited to that which is given by the physical world through the five senses. But in the Jungian schema there is also the mysterious presence of evil, which has a spiritual origin through which it touches the human being directly and also is found spread through the physical world (just as we find evidence of God's presence in the physical world). Jung also suggested that there are organizing principles within the psychoid realm—both within human beings and outside of them—which he calls *archetypes*. These can have a great impact upon those human beings who are energized by them.

Jung's first and most important change in the Freudian system was to claim that while we are indeed physical creatures, we are also in touch with, surrounded by, and a part of a meaningful spiritual, nonphysical dimension of reality. He wrote to me: "We know as little of supreme being as of matter. But there is as little doubt of the existence of supreme being as of matter. *The world beyond is a reality,* an experiential fact."[4] And this nonphysical world is not meaningless or subhuman, as Freud believed; rather, it contains an advocate, a helper who wishes to bring human beings to wholeness, to salvation. Jung called this *das Selbst,* the itself, a reality superior to the human being. In *Psychology and Alchemy* (Princeton, 1968), his study of *das Selbst,* Jung stated that the idea that the human psyche contains layers *below* and *inferior* to human consciousness bothers no one, but we consider it a crime of high treason against human nature to suggest there can be something *superior* to human beings that is trying to help them. Yet that is exactly what he experienced as he looked deeply into his own soul and the souls of others. Jung also pointed out that it is only a tiny fraction of humanity, those who live in the heavily populated peninsula of Eurasia that juts out into the Atlantic and think that they are "cultured" who have proposed the idea that "religion is a peculiar kind of mental disturbance of undiscoverable purport."[5]

Jung felt that religion was necessary for human development, and he could not imagine why people could not understand that he was speaking of a real, nonphysical dimension of reality when he spoke of the human psyche and the spiritual realm from which it issued. He wrote in a letter: "I did not create the psyche. If we speak of God as an archetype, we say nothing about His real nature, but are letting it be known that God already has a place in that part of the psyche which is pre-existent to consciousness, and that therefore He cannot be considered an invention of consciousness. We neither make Him nor remove or eliminate Him, but bring Him closer to the possibility of being experienced."[6] God's Spirit has its foothold in the human soul, and so the psalmist cries out to God not to take away his Holy Spirit. Knowledge is not confined to the five senses; we human beings share in spiritual reality, and we can have direct experience of God and other spiritual realities existing there. It took me nearly 10 years of working with some of Jung's followers to break out of my materialism and realize what Jung was saying, and to realize that his view on this subject was similiar to that of Jesus of Nazareth.

The second major change that Jung made in Freud's schema was to suggest that the psyche is not an organized system of self-deception, but that through revelations, visions, intuitions, dreams, gifts of healing, knowledge, wisdom, and other experiences we are given genuine knowledge of this other dimension of reality. Modern neurophysiology of dreaming supports Jung in his contention that the space-time distortion in dreams is not created by a psychic process. We are also given the gifts of discernment to help decide what is of God and what is not. Along with most of the church Fathers, Jung believed that something wiser than we speaks through our dreams. Unlike Freud, Jung did not believe that the messages of the unconscious had been scrambled by a censor; he claimed,

rather, that we have forgotten how to understand the language
of symbolism. As we learn the meaning of symbols in the
Bible, in the parables of Jesus, in art and literature and drama,
we can begin to understand our dreams.

In addition, Jung became convinced that the human psyche
contains many more drives than those for sex and power. So
he made a third change in Freud's system. He believed that
unless we come into touch with God, we are likely to become
neurotic. We have already quoted Jung's statement that neurosis is a religious matter and that the church as well as psychiatrists and psychologists should be helping people with their
psychological problems. Jung also believed that the full dogma
and practice of the Christian church was the best therapeutic
system ever given to human beings; he maintained that real
Christianity deals with whole people, and that through its dogmatic beliefs and religious rituals and practices it enables us
to avoid the "curse of pathology."[7]

In his book *Psychotherapy and the Cure of Souls in Jung's
Psychology* Hans Schaer provided an excellent analysis of
Jung's attitude toward Christianity, both Catholic and Protestant. Schaer was a close friend of Jung's and a minister of
the Swiss Reformed Church. In the chapter entitled "Man and
Religion" he sketched out Jung's deep admiration of Catholicism and then Jung's attitude toward Protestantism. Jung believed that the Catholicism of his time provided human beings
the best objectivication of the total unconscious (and therefore
the greatest psychotherapeutic help) of any religious system—
superior to Eastern religions just because these symbols were
seen as part of the objective, real outer world. He also believed
that Protestantism stripped Westerners of their symbols and
forced them into a confrontation with the unconscious for
which they were not ready.

Jung's thinking contains one major flaw. He assumed that
an individual is either inside the dogmatic system where the

symbols have meaning and saving power, or outside of it and unable ever to reenter. My experience is that we can be outside the naive acceptance of dogma and still find that the symbols have saving power. Paul Ricoeur calls this *the second naivete.* Jung seldom acknowledged this possibility.

A fourth change that Jung made in Freud's thought was to give an alternative to the notion of an innate death wish. Jung proposed that just as there is a healing reality that seeks to bring us to wholeness (what Christians call God or the risen Christ or the Holy Spirit), there is also a destructive force that tries to pull us down into its own destructiveness.* Jung saw evil as a reality both within and beyond the human psyche, a reality that tries to cripple us. Radical evil needs to be distinguished from our personal human shadow, which may consist of good parts of ourselves that we have repressed and that we need to face and deal with. Essential evil cannot be handled by human beings alone, but only with the intervention of God or, as Christians would say, by the risen Christ who has already defeated evil. One part of Jung's thought therefore came close to the early church's idea of evil. The Fathers called evil *Death* and believed that it affected human beings in four ways: morally in sin, psychologically in demonic possession and mental illness, physically in sickness and disability, and finally in physical death itself.

Jung's framework is similar to that of the New Testament and the teachings of Jesus; it is the framework implied in Jesus' death and rising, and in the teachings and practice of the early church.

---

*Jung's writing about evil is ambiguous. At times as in *The Answer to Job* he portrayed evil as a part of God, while in *Aion* (Princeton, 1968) he made no reference to this idea. John Sanford has pointed out to me passages in the second volume of his *Letters* (Princeton, 1973, pp. 120, 134, 494-5) supporting the former idea. However, there is no suggestion of this idea in the passage equating God with love that we will quote in a few pages. In *Aion* and other places evil is seen as a radical and destructive force apart from God.

I am deeply grateful to Jung and his followers. Years ago I found myself a Christian minister still caught in a materialistic world view with no real belief in the world of spirit. But if I believed that there was no world of the spirit or that we cannot be in touch with it, then what I professed as a Christian consciously was being denied by my unconscious assumption. When I listened carefully in the middle of the night, I heard the dark voice telling me that I didn't really believe what I was saying, that I was split in two, that I was a fraud. Such an attitude is very uncomfortable; it is the stuff of which neurosis is made.

When I found myself in this condition, none of my Christian colleagues were in a position to help. It was Jung who provided me with a reasonable world view in which the reality of Jesus' incarnation, life, death, resurrection, and ascension, and the giving of the Holy Spirit made sense. Jung was not the Savior, but he released me from the materialistic box in which I had been imprisoned; he gave me the freedom to let the full saving power of the risen Jesus begin a process of transformation in me. And yet during my visit with Jung I asked him which psychological approach was closest to his own method. Instead of naming a psychologist he replied: "The spiritual directors in France in the late 19th century—people like Abbé Huvelin."

I am not a Jungian, but a Christian for whom Jung opened the door out of the materialistic prison of which William James spoke. (Even Jung himself, by the way, once remarked that he was glad that he was Jung and not a Jungian.) I am deeply grateful for Jung's help, but at the same time I see clearly that Jung is not the whole answer. He can only open the door; he does not bring us into the presence of the saving One. When I visited with Jung, he told me that both theologians and medical doctors misunderstood him. He said that he was simply a psychiatrist, a doctor of the soul, who had found that both the spiritual domain and the saving power available there were real, and that we human beings could not come to our full potential if we did not take these realities into consideration. It was not his task, Jung thought, to be a minister or priest. He once begged the great Anglican theologian Archbishop William Temple to send him clergy to train so that they could bring about this integration of theology and psychology.

When Jung himself theologized, however, as he did in several of his books, he sometimes showed a lack of good historical understanding of theology and Christianity. He also never told readers when he was discussing an issue about which he had changed his mind, so readers have to know when a given book was written in order to understand whether it represents Jung's mature and final understanding of the subject. His books, furthermore, are often difficult, because Jung had a wide European education, read both Greek and Latin fluently, and knew most of modern psychological and scientific thought—and he expected his readers to know just as much! He also expected readers to know their Freud, and to know that—except in regard to the specific issues he disagreed with—he accepted the Freudian framework. In addition, Jung was not a systematic thinker. We have already indicated his ambiguity about evil. He gave his deepest and best understanding of a subject at the time of writing. Sometimes his succeeding interpretations differed. Like the Bible, Jung must be interpreted, and there are differing interpretations.

But the greatest problem that Christians have in reading Jung is that Jung is ambivalent about institutional Christianity and about its belief in the resurrection of Jesus and its saving power. He was raised by a father who was a minister in the Swiss Reformed Church. Evidently his father's intellectual faith was not very secure, and he expected his son to accept faith on authority, without discussion. Jung was a deeply religious boy and young man, but he was scarred by this relationship. So even though Jung thought of himself as a Christian, he did not see the importance for himself of the saving action of Jesus' death and resurrection. In *Memories, Dreams, Reflections* (Pantheon, 1963) Jung described a vision he had at age 64, when he was writing his book *Psychology and Religion* and working on a seminar concerned with Ignatius of Loyola's *Spiritual Exercises:*

> One night I awoke and saw, bathed in bright light at the foot of my bed, the figure of Christ on the Cross. It was not quite life-size, but extremely distinct; and I saw that his body was made of greenish gold. The vision was marvelously beautiful, and yet I was profoundly shaken by it. . . .
>
> If I had not been so struck by the greenish-gold, I would have been tempted to assume that something essential was missing from my "Christian" view—in other words, that my traditional Christ-image was somehow inadequate and that I still had to catch up with part of the Christian development. The emphasis on the metal, however, showed me the undisguised alchemical conception of Christ as a union of spiritually alive and physically dead matter.[8]

It is notoriously difficult to interpret one's own dreams, and I wonder along with Vera van der Heydt if he did not fail to get the real message of the dream, the message that he was "tempted to assume." In her lecture, *Jung and Religion,* van der Heydt relates that following his father's death Jung "had to leave the room if anyone mentioned Jesus or Christ. . . . From childhood on he feared and distrusted Jesus . . . . This was also a great secret which Jung had to keep from his parents. This fear of Jesus and his resistance against the all-goodness and lightness of Christ remained with Jung all through his life."[9] In addition often he referred to the incarnation in his writing, but almost never to the resurrection of Jesus. Jung simply avoided this central tenet of the Christian faith. One can accept the basic philosophical and psychological ideas of Jung without accepting his opinion on a subject that he never fully examined.[10]

In spite of all this, Jung concluded his chapter entitled "Late Thoughts" in his autobiography with these words: "Man can try to name love, showering upon it all the names at his command, but still he will involve himself in endless self-deceptions. If he possesses a grain of wisdom, he will lay down his arms and name the unknown by the more unknown, *ignotum per ignotius*—that is, by the name of God. That is a confession of his subjection, his imperfection, and his dependence; but at the same time a testimony to his freedom to choose between truth and error."[11] This is the same conclusion reached by some of the greatest Christian saints. I think that part of Jung was far more Christian than he himself knew.[12]

Richard Coan, a professor of psychology at the University of Arizona, has spent a large part of his professional career seeking to determine the nature of the optimal human personality; he has provided a survey of his findings in his book *Hero, Artist, Sage or Saint?: A Survey of Views on What Is Variously Called Mental Health, Normality, Maturity, Self-Actualization, and Human Fulfillment* (Columbia, 1977). Coan began his book by stating that psychology as a science cannot provide the goals for human life. He claimed that if any goals *are* provided by psychology, the psychologists must either drag them in surreptitiously through the back door or openly acknowledge the need for religion and transpersonal meaning.

Coan concluded that there are five elements that characterize the fully developed human person: efficiency, creativity, inner harmony, relatedness, and transcendence. (Some thinkers and societies, he pointed out, emphasize one or two of these to the neglect of others.) Coan described these elements.

1. Efficiency is the heroic quality. Heroes accomplish things with effectiveness, have strong egos, and are able to focus the direction of their lives. Jung remarked that psychotics may have great religious experiences, but they are unable to do anything with them; the truly religious person, however, not

only needs experiences of the risen Christ but also needs to be an effective instrument of that power in the world. This heroism can be embodied in outer actions, in thinking, in scientific discovery, in religious practice, or in theological study.

2. The creative person, so often represented by the artist, is able to present images, poetry, or ideas in a new way so that they touch others with a dimension beyond the physical. Of course, there is little real art without discipline, and the greatest art (as found in Dante's *Divine Comedy,* for example) usually touches the transcendent and transpersonal.

3. The sage is one who has come to inner harmony. According to Coan, one goal of life is to reduce the tension and fear and conflict within us, and to come to harmony. This harmony can be found either by obliterating upsetting emotions or by finding a reality that gives inner peace even amid the pain and brokenness of this life.

4. The saint is one who treats others with understanding, caring, love, empathy, social sensitivity, compassion. Saints make other people feel loved. Christian sainthood is certainly characterized by "loving one another as I have loved you." Coan quoted James Baldwin's statement of the world's need for such saintliness: "The moment we cease to hold each other, the moment we break faith with one another, the sea engulfs us and the light goes out."

5. Relatedness is the horizontal dimension of saintliness, and transcendence is its vertical aspect. Relatedness becomes intolerable unless we are empowered from above. Clergy burn-out occurs when religious professionals try to live the Christian life without the empowerment supplied by prayer. In its hunger for true caring the world swallows and destroys us if we are not given divine support. Life burns out, falls apart, and loses its meaning if we have no experience of a God who reaches down, touches us, and draws us into the transcendental dimension both now and at death; indeed, sometimes our ex-

perience of transcendence is actually a sense of being saved from the forces of evil within and around us.

Coan suggested that Jung, as thoroughly as any modern psychologist, gave consideration to each of these elements of human wholeness and developed a framework in which they all have a place. This has also been my experience, after reading psychology for 30 years. And as I listen to the message of Jesus of Nazareth and the church built on his resurrection, I hear the affirmation of these elements as essential features of the full Christian life.

Dr. Roy Fairchild has suggested still another way of determining what kind of psychology will augment Christian ministry in his penetrating article in *Phos* (Christmas 1984, p. 3), a magazine of theological reflections. Dr. Fairchild is professor of Spiritual Life and Psychology at San Francisco Theological Seminary and in the Graduate Theological Union of Berkeley, California. He offers five questions that need to be asked of any psychological system before it is used to implement the Christian outreach toward other people.

1. Does this psychology deal with the basic, existential questions of life, such as freedom, death, isolation, meaninglessness? What can I trust? How do we know? What kind of life is worth living? As the former president of the American Psychological Association, Ernest Hilgard, has said: ". . . These are not trivial 'academic' questions. . . . On the contrary, they center upon the most vital motives and forces underlying Western thought and civilization . . . ."

2. Does this psychology recognize the person's symbolic world as crucial in self-understanding? Symbols and images are gadflies that lure the person forward in hope or backward in despair. We need a psychology which takes into account the pull of expectancies and images as well as the push of drives and tensions.

3. Does this psychology investigate empathy, compassion, and love with as much vigor as it does autonomy and self-

realization? Empathy, the capacity of a person to feel the needs, aspirations, joys and sorrows, anxieties and hurt of others as if they were his or her own, is a very neglected field in psychology.

4. Does this psychology see the person as having some genuine freedom and not as a helpless victim of external circumstances, caught in a deterministic trap? Christopher Lasch concludes that: "A genuine affirmation of the self . . . insists on a core of selfhood not subject to environmental determination, even under extreme conditions. Self-affirmation remains a possibility precisely to the degree that an older conception of personality, rooted in Judaeo-Christian traditions, has persisted alongside a behavioral or therapeutic conception" (*The Minimal Self* [New York: W.W. Norton, 1984], p. 59).

5. Does this psychology seek to comprehend ego-transcending as well as ego-enhancing experience? Is mysticism taken seriously? Is there an excessive concern with self-image, whether positive or negative? Eastern and Western spiritual traditions hold that egocentricity and the importance of the self-image must steadily be decreased, that we must die to any image of self we cling to. Gerald May's conviction is that: "A contemplative approach (to psychology) must find a way of getting beyond this preoccupation; somehow one must come to let one's evaluations be, and move through them until the images of self can be seen for what they are—images" (*Will and Spirit* [San Francisco: Harper and Row, 1982], p. 105).

Hopefully, these questions may allow us to discern where we are likely to draw wisdom for our ministries from that disciplined curiosity about human nature called psychology.[13]

These questions go to the heart of the matter. Once again, Jung dealt with all of them, although as we have noted he did not deal with the transcendent event of Jesus' resurrection as Christians do. Let us see what support can be given for the more open universe to which both Christianity and Jung bear witness.

3

LIVING IN AN OPEN UNIVERSE

The preceding chapters have presented a view of reality and of human beings that perceives us as very complicated beings with capabilities of dealing with a complex world in which spirit and matter are real and in which God and evil are realities. When we do not deal with this total reality as consciously as possible, we can either fall into psychological or physical illness, or become controlled by negative forces of which we are often not aware (the condition usually called "sin" by the church). When we do not use our capacities as fully as possible, we cannot avoid aspects of reality that may be damaging to us. Nor can we find the Savior who can rescue us from disaster, the one who can bring us abundant life.

Why is it so difficult for human beings in our age to hear this message and respond to it? There are many reasons, but two are vitally important. The first is psychological; the second is philosophical and relates to our world view. Both reasons, however, are probably related.

Most of us have within us infantile expectations that we never entirely outgrow. Deep within us there still lurks the egocentricity of the infant, who assumes three things: "(1) I am in control or ought to be in control of all that has to do with life; (2) I am at the center of the universe; (3) Everything and everyone ought to be spinning around me so I can have what I want and life will be the way I want it to be."[1] This inner infantile "king" wants to run the universe rather than seek a Savior who is already running it and who can help us achieve our destiny in that universe. Dr. Harry Tiebout, the expert on alcoholism, has suggested that these assumptions are not only expectations but also delusions. Until alcoholics can begin to give up these attitudes, Tiebout discovered, they cannot get over their addiction. Most of us have our less obvious addictions, and we cannot begin to let the loving and redeeming God transform our lives in any truly effective way until we see the necessity of giving up such infantile attitudes. We are converted or born again when we begin to surrender these attitudes and turn to God. This can happen to us again and again as we surrender more and more of ourselves to God.

There is a second, more philosophical, reason why many people find it difficult to imagine the view of the universe and of human beings proposed by Christianity. Most of us have been totally immersed in a world view that is entirely materialistic, leaving no place for spirit. And this world view has taken over our Western world—its culture, its thinking, its living, its academic institutions, its governments, and even many of its churches. This materialism has its roots in the thinking of Aristotle, who stated that we humans have no direct contact with a spiritual world; according to Aristotelian thought, we are limited to experiences of the five senses (with which we explore the knowable, physical world) and to reason (with which we make logical deductions and inferences about reality). The beliefs of Aristotle became the foundation for both Protestant and Catholic scholasticism. And the 18th-century Enlightenment, following the lead of Thomas Hobbes, went even farther, with an outright denial of the existence of anything but the physical world.

In the next century that followed, the dramatic successes of physics, chemistry, medicine, and other hard sciences convinced many thinkers that science had the final truth about *all reality,* and that the spiritual world was indeed pure illusion. This point of view can be presented in a very simple line drawing that is quite different from the diagrams we have already presented.

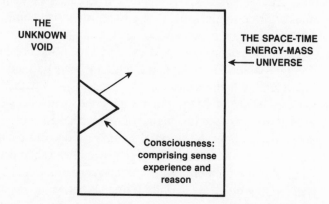

THE
UNKNOWN
VOID

THE SPACE-TIME
ENERGY-MASS
◄——UNIVERSE

Consciousness:
comprising sense
experience and
reason

According to this diagram, the entire knowable world consists of the central box, the limited space-time, energy-mass world. Human consciousness or knowing is a strange anomaly, somehow introduced into the box but of no ultimate significance. Both the psychobiologists and the behaviorists reduce even our knowing to the interaction of purely physical particles; their ideas are simply the logical result of this world view.

This point of view is so much a part of us Westerners that we fail to see how it affects nearly every part of our lives. Recently I had a class for religious professionals in which six of the ten class members were educated, Asian pastors, and it was difficult for them to believe that most Western people really held to such a constricted viewpoint. If this view of reality is correct, then the view of Jesus, which we presented in our last chapter, is sheer nonsense. God, the spiritual world, afterlife, resurrection, salvation, grace, the gifts of the Spirit, and the eternal value of love, as well as sin and evil, must be merely illusory ideas which allow human beings to delude themselves into believing that there is some meaning in existence.

Indeed, from the materialistic viewpoint, these ideas can even be seen as dangerous delusions. Freud described them as manifestations of an infantile desire to return to the womb. (If Freud were the only depth psychologist, I would have to reject the idea of the unconscious.) Marx called them the opiate of the people, which keeps human beings in bondage, and liberation theology bothers me, for I do not see any way that the basic materialism of Marx can be integrated into the world view of Jesus and what he taught. In many Marxist states it is illegal to teach about the spiritual world or God. But even in non-Marxist, Western countries there is usually a subtle denial of spiritual reality in journalism, TV, and academic education, as well as in politics and in daily living. What we do tends to be a better indication of what we believe than what we declare we believe.

In his book *Twentieth Century Religious Thought* (Scribner, 1981), John Macquarrie examined some 140 religious thinkers whom he considered to have been most important between 1900 and 1960. Only two of them had any place for an experience of God (Jung and von Hügel), and most of them were basically trying to fit Christianity into a materialistic framework. They assumed that this understanding of reality was the only possible one for educated modern people. Later we shall point out the shortcomings of this point of view.

How congenial this view of the world is to the egocentricity that we described above! From the materialistic viewpoint, there is nothing higher than human beings. The world around us is just a thing, and if we are logical behaviorists or bio-geneticists, then people are also just things. They can be used, manipulated, exploited, or exterminated, just like any other thing. If I am trapped in this viewpoint, my goal is simply to assert my own will and power and to gain as many of the world's goods as I can before inevitable extinction. Within this framework, those who follow the religious way are considered to be weak, as Nietzsche suggested, or suffering from a compulsive neurosis, or really deluded. Obviously, then, what we truly believe at the gut level about the world and human beings makes a great deal of difference in how we behave.

Eastern Idealism

Many people in the West have come to realize the futility of this view of reality, and they have turned to the only alternative they know, Eastern religions, as a way out of their blind alley. (Christian Science is the only homemade American religious framework that goes along with the East in viewing the physical world as illusion and only the world of spirit as real.) A trip from New Delhi to Agra in the middle of the summer on a road swarming with people and animals gave me an understanding of why Buddha wanted to get off the world. When the physical world seems intolerable, meaningless, or unchangeable, there is always the temptation to deny its existence and to retreat into our inner worlds where such things as spirit, psyche, and God are the only reality. This predominantly Eastern point of view can also be sketched out in a simple line drawing.

In this world view, the mirror-opposite of Western materialism, it is the physical world that is illusory; the ego that helps

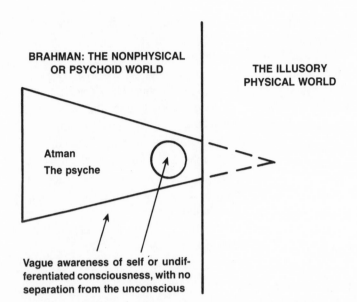

**BRAHMAN: THE NONPHYSICAL
OR PSYCHOID WORLD**

**THE ILLUSORY
PHYSICAL WORLD**

**Atman
The psyche**

**Vague awareness of self or undif-
ferentiated consciousness, with no
separation from the unconscious**

us get around in that world is also illusion. The spiritual, psychoid, or nonphysical world *alone* is real. One becomes mature
as one recognizes that only spirit is real and that there is little
distinction between one's individual spirit and Spirit. In Hindu
terms, we first come to realize the ground of our individual
existence, Atman, and then we realize that it is identical with
the ground of all reality, Brahman.

I have found the world view espoused by Jesus, the early
church, Plato, and Jung to be a much more satisfactory alternative to materialism than Eastern or Western Idealism, in
which only the nonphysical is real. Within a system based on
Idealism, salvation is usually achieved by our own conscious
effort. Many people find it difficult, however, to imagine
meaningful existence except as an experience of being saved
again and again from their brokenness and failure. In his book

Gandhi, Portrayal of a Friend (Abingdon, 1983), E. Stanley Jones clearly pointed out this basic difference between his Christianity and Gandhi's Hinduism. Jones noted that while Gandhi concentrated on his own spiritual discipline, Christianity stresses unmerited salvation.

In addition, there is within the Eastern world view—either in Hinduism or Buddhism—little motivation for attempting to be instruments of the transforming love that Jesus incarnated. I am troubled, for example, by a statement made by the god Krishna in the *Bhagavad-Gita*. Arjuna, the Hindu scripture's hero, faces the battle rank of his foes with his own army and realizes that there are many relatives and friends in the opposing forces. He tells Krishna, who stands beside him, that he does not want to go out into battle and slaughter them. Krishna tells him, though, that they are only illusion, and admonishes him to do his duty—to kill them.

I doubt that the Eastern way is an adequate alternative to Western materialism. It is, however, certainly a more hopeful and meaningful view of human existence than materialism, particularly when the theoretical viewpoint is enriched by the wisdom and spiritual discipline of the leaders of these great religions. But Jung warned Western people that following this Eastern way can be very dangerous. Many Westerners try to take over this religious framework without the stringent discipline required by Eastern masters, and their identification of Atman and Brahman can lead, ironically, to the same egocentricity that is so congenial to materialism. Even in Japan there is a sickness known as Zen madness, which frequently causes people to become detached from this world, yet never to pass through the prison of deluding images to *satori*. Those who have not spent much time in the Orient can hardly imagine the pervasiveness of such a world view. In fact, though, it is likely that more people base their lives on it than upon materialism.

We cannot bring the Christian message to them unless we have a sympathetic understanding of their beliefs.

Several modern scientists have turned to this Eastern world view after discovering how different physical reality is from what they had thought it to be and after realizing that the human psyche can influence the world of physical events. In his Clifford Lectures in 1927, entitled *The Nature of the Physical World* (Darby, 1981), Sir Arthur Eddington proposed a view of reality as idea or Spirit. In his many books Alfred North Whitehead also delineated a very sophisticated metaphysical system that seeks to avoid the problems of seeing matter and spirit as different realities. And one of the most recent of these attempts by Western scientists to describe spiritual reality is that of Fritjof Capra, entitled *The Tao of Physics* (Bantam, 1977).

None of these thinkers, however, has taken seriously the basic viewpoint of Jesus, who undoubtedly believed that there were two interacting dimensions of reality, physical and non-physical, both created by God and both good. The whole idea of the incarnation also speaks of the goodness of the physical world. If we believe that Jesus, as God incarnate, shared both a divine and human nature—as the Council of Chalcedon proclaimed so many centuries ago—then his understanding of the universe and of human nature is one to be taken very seriously. Jesus, in other words, was an important philosopher and theologian as well as a moralist. When we listen to Jesus of Nazareth through the insights of the best thinking of modern physics and psychology, we realize that he has something of incredible value to offer in both of these disciplines. It is important, therefore, to look at evidence available in our modern world of the spiritual reality described and exemplified by Jesus, evidence not gained through ordinary sense experience.

The Evidence for a Wider Knowledge of Reality

Are there any objective data that human beings actually experience God or some nonphysical dimension of existence? There are several important sociological studies of such experience. One of the most important was a research project undertaken by the National Opinion Research Center under a grant from the Henry Luce Foundation. Some 1,460 people were selected in a random national sample and were interviewed. Andrew Greeley, a sociologist as well as a novelist, was responsible for the study, and he reported the findings in *The Sociology of the Paranormal: A Reconnaissance.*[2] The goal of the project was to discover whether Americans indeed had paranormal experiences, including mystical experiences. The group working with Greeley defined the term *mystical* by using William James' four categories of religious experience: *noetic* (did it provide knowledge?), *ineffable* (was it as indescribable as any other basic experience?), *passive* (was it given rather than created?), and *transient* (did the experience pass, as most experiences do?).

When the computers began to spit out the results, the investigators were astonished to find that 39% of their sample replied yes to the question, "Have you ever felt as though you were very close to a powerful, spiritual force that seemed to lift you out of yourself?" When they did some post-test rechecks to verify these data, they discovered that half of this 39% had never told anyone of their experiences, because they did not wish to receive the derision of a society that believes only in the physical world. According to the study, the last people to whom most of them would turn for an explanation of these experiences were the professionals in the churches, because they felt that the clergy did not believe in such things anymore.

Greeley anticipated that critics would suggest that these peo-

ple were unstable or immature, so he had his researchers build
into the questionnaire the Bradburn-Caplovitz psychological
well-being scale. The results showed a high correlation between direct experience of God and psychological well-being
or emotional maturity—a fact that soundly contradicts the spec-
ulations of both Freud and Marx. But if, indeed, the world
view that Jesus suggested is correct, then these results are what
we would expect; the individuals who describe such spiritual
experiences have been touched by the source of meaning in
the universe. The survey also revealed that those who claimed
to have experienced God also tended to believe in an afterlife
and were in general hopeful and optimistic about life. Indeed,
Professor Norman Bradburn commented at a staff meeting of
the National Opinion Research Center that he knew of no other
variable that correlated as strongly with psychological well-
being as does frequent religious experience. Other researchers
in mysticism have noted the same correlation as John R. Finney
pointed out to me.[3]

The researchers on this project also asked the question,
"Have you ever felt that you were really in touch with someone
who had died?" Of their sample 27% answered in the affirm-
ative, and again these people also scored high on the emotional-
maturity scale.

Another study by Richard Kalish and David Reynolds, fi-
nanced by a grant from the National Institute of Mental Health
and reported in the *Journal for the Scientific Study of Religion,*
discovered that 44% of a methodically selected sample—including blacks, Japanese-Americans, Mexican-Americans, and
whites—claimed to have experienced the presence of someone
who had died.[4] Most interesting in Kalish's and Reynolds'
study was their report that when they looked for other sociological studies of such experience, they found *none*. Of course,
if we assume that the physical universe is all that exists, it is

a nonquestion to ask if there is survival outside of the body. What questions we ask and what we look for will be determined basically by what we believe. It is not surprising, therefore, that in 1975 Greeley also found few other sociological studies of religious experience.

But many Christians do report this kind of experience. In his book *Angels: God's Secret Agents* (Pocket Books, 1976), Billy Graham told of several examples of Christian people experiencing the deceased. In *Ring of Truth: A Translator's Testimony* (Shaw, 1977), J. B. Phillips told of his vision of C. S. Lewis after Lewis had died. I have given other examples of this kind of Christian experience in my book *Afterlife*. It should be noted that all of these encounters or visions were spontaneously given; they were not sought. It is one thing graciously to receive what is given and still another to use spiritualistic methods of trying to obtain them; the latter can get people in serious trouble. And even these spontaneous happenings need to be subjected to the gift of discernment of the Christian community.

In addition to his other startling findings, Greeley discovered that human beings seem to be able to get information quite naturally through methods other than the five ordinary senses. Of his sample 59% had experiences of *déjà vu,* of thinking that they had been somewhere before, while simultaneously realizing that they could not have been. Furthermore, 58% had experiences of telepathy, of feeling in touch with someone far away. And 24% had experiences of clairvoyance, seeing events that were happening at a great distance precisely at the time when they were happening.

Greeley's data were verified by D. Hay and A. Morisy from the Religious Experience Unit, Manchester College, Oxford, which reported its findings in October of 1977. Substantially the same results were obtained by a group in Germany. And even though much of the scientific community ignores these fields of study, excellent work has been done at the Stanford Research Institute and at Princeton University.[5] (Again I want to make it clear that it is quite different to study the fact that human beings naturally have such experiences and another to try to obtain these experiences in strange ways that build up our egocentricity.)

If indeed there is a nonphysical, spiritual world that surrounds us and filters into material reality, a world in which our own souls exist, then we have to make quite an effort to avoid it. Nonetheless, our lack of belief in such a reality can limit our experience of it. An experiment at the cognitive learning laboratories at Harvard shows how difficult it is to deal with experiences that are contrary to what we believe about the world. Postman and Bruner devised an experiment to test what they called "cognitive dissonance," our inability to perceive what does not fit into our accepted mode of belief. They took a black six of spades from an ordinary deck of playing cards and had it painted red. The card was then reinserted in the deck, and the deck was shown to a large number of subjects. Practically none of them saw the red six of spades as a *red six of spades*. They reported seeing either an ordinary black six of spades or a six of diamonds or hearts. They did not "see" what was actually there, because what was presented to them did not fit their belief system about a deck of cards.

Similarly, those who are totally caught in a materialistic world view do not believe what they are experiencing when something occurs that does not fit into that framework; if it is possible to block out objective sensory data, how much easier to reject inner experiences such as those described by Greeley and others. Indeed, in *The Structure of Scientific Revolutions* (Univ. of Chicago, 1970), T. S. Kuhn reminded us that most of the important scientific discoveries have been made by young scientists or people coming into a field where they were not "brainwashed" by accepted theory. Einstein was a high-school dropout.

The best minds on the cutting edge of physics have, in fact, come to doubt the adequacy of the materialistic view of the universe. In his Gifford Lectures, published under the title *Physics and Philosophy: The Revolution in Modern Science* (Harper & Row, 1958), Werner Heisenberg—one of the greatest revolutionaries in modern science—stated that science had become so skeptical that it was even skeptical of its own skepticism and had discarded many of the ideas that it once considered final and certain. I quote his impressive statement:

> One of the most important features of the development and analysis of modern physics is the experience that the concepts of natural language, vaguely defined as they are, seem to be more stable in the expansion of knowledge than the precise terms of scientific language, derived as an idealization from only limited groups of phenomena. This is in fact not surprising since the concepts of natural language are formed by the immediate connection with reality; they represent reality. . . .
>
> Keeping in mind the intrinsic stability of the concepts of natural language in the process of scientific development, one sees that—after the experience of modern physics—our attitude toward concepts like mind or the human soul or life or God will be different from that of the nineteenth century, because these concepts belong to the natural language and have therefore immediate connection with reality.[6]

Heisenberg's reflections were published in 1958. Since then physics has continued to make gigantic strides in understanding the world in which we live. The physical universe now appears even less mechanical and less probably the result of chance than it did 30 years ago. Quantum mechanics shows clearly that we conscious observers exert an influence on our physical world as we observe it. We do indeed live in an open and mysterious universe, as Paul Davies pointed out in his book *God and the New Physics* (Simon and Schuster, 1984). Davies did not take into consideration the data of religious experience that many people consider the most significant data in knowing about God and our world. However, he did show that a review of quantum mechanics and other bizarre concepts of modern physics leaves little room for a simplistic materialism or for a chance (accidental) theory of this universe of which we are a part.[7]

The work of Kurt Gödel, described by Nagel and Newman in *Gödel's Proof* (NYU, 1958), shows that even mathematics does not give absolute certainty. In 1933, as a young man of only 27, Gödel detected some flaws in what was then considered the final word in mathematical theory, *Principia Mathematica* (Cambridge, 1910) by Russell and Whitehead. Using Russell and Whitehead's own methods, Gödel demonstrated that two quite different answers can be obtained from the same group of mathematical data. The implications of this discovery, which has been replicated in various ways by several other mathematicians, are most impressive. If we cannot be sure about our mathematics, then we cannot be absolutely certain about any scientific theory. A friend of mine who is a computer programmer has pointed out to me that since computers operate on the very principles of mathematics that Gödel has called into question, they sometimes produce completely extraneous answers. Probably only God has absolute certainty about anything.

Gödel believed that mathematical concepts are perceived by intuition in the same way that Plato thought that the ideas were grasped. If it is true that even our mathematical reasoning can be faulty and needs to be checked against reality and experience, how much more must we be wary of rational speculation and metaphysics that soar off into intellectual fantasy. It is important to remind ourselves that even the most logical "proofs" are never certain. So those who try to *reason* God out of existence cannot be taken any more seriously than those who try to reason him *into* reality. Only when we encounter and are transformed by the living God do we truly know that we live in a meaningful universe, that there is an Other who cares for us and seeks us out to shower love upon us.

In my book *Encounter with God* (Bethany, 1972), I traced the history of how the Western world came to believe that physical atoms of various sizes and shapes are the only reality. I described how, according to this theory, these atoms operated on the mechanical principles devised by Sir Isaac Newton to produce our entire universe, and then developed into human beings through the blind, random, natural selection Darwin spoke of. But the theory, I argued, began to break down when scientists found that atoms—far from being substantial—are made up of hundreds of subatomic particles that behave more like electrical charges and wave patterns than like "things." Newton's laws, furthermore, have been shown by Einstein and Heisenberg not to be universally applicable. And finally the work of Pierre Teilhard de Chardin, Loren Eiseley, and many others has forced scientists to consider the possibility that there is more than blind chance operating in biological and human development.

The only way materialists can prove that there is no world of spirit is by demonstrating that they know everything about everything—and that is an absurd attitude for any human being to take. Or, more modestly, they could show that their theory explains all available data, and that there is, as a result, no need for a belief in spirit. We are, however, finding more and more data that we cannot explain by materialistic theories. So strict materialists, who maintain that there is no spirit or God, are placing themselves in an absurd position, trying to prove a negative hypothesis—that something does not exist. Anyone who tries to sustain such a position usually falls into one of the two absurd assumptions of egomania that we have just mentioned.

The Evidence of Medicine

Some years ago Flanders Dunbar, a young woman teaching medicine at Columbia University Medical School, collected all the information she could find indicating that emotions have an effect on physical functioning. Her book *Emotions and Bodily Changes* inaugurated a new era in medicine and stimulated the development of psychosomatic medicine. In her book she quoted an article published in the 1920s by a British physician, F. G. Crookshank, in which the author described the absurd extreme to which sheerly physiological healing techniques are liable to go:

> I often wonder that some hardboiled and orthodox clinician does not describe emotional weeping as a "new disease," calling it paroxysmal lachrymation, and suggesting treatment by belladonna, astringent local applications, avoidance of sexual excess, tea, tobacco and alcohol, and a salt-free diet with restriction of fluid intake, proceeding in the event of failure to early removal of the tear glands.[8]

Few people but behaviorists would suggest that religion can have no effect on *mature* human beings. Once we see how emotions can affect every part of the body, we can readily understand how religious faith and experience can affect our physical as well as our emotional health. Dr. Jerome Frank, a professor of psychiatry at Johns Hopkins Medical School, concluded his book *Persuasion and Healing* with these words:

> The question of how far a physician should go to meet a patient's expectations is a thorny one. Obviously he cannot use methods

in which he himself does not believe. Moreover, reliance on the healing powers of faith, if it led to neglect of proper diagnostic or treatment procedures, would clearly be irresponsible. On the other hand, faith may be a specific antidote for certain emotions such as fear or discouragement, which may constitute the essence of a patient's illness. For such patients, the mobilization of expectant trust by whatever means may be as much an etiological remedy as penicillin for pneumonia.[9]

A few years ago Dr. Candace Pert was part of the team that discovered the opiate receptors in the brain that led to the discovery of the endorphins. These chemicals produced by the body are more powerful painkillers than any known opiates; they also can have a regenerating effect on the human body. And they can be released by the faith of the individual, the expectant trust that he or she does not live in a meaningless universe, but rather in a universe in which the individual is cared about. In Chapter 4 of my book *Prophetic Ministry* (Crossroad, 1982), I analyzed the notion of faith and detailed some of the information recently discovered concerning its central position in the facilitation of both physical well-being and psychological health.

Herbert Benson, a Harvard M.D., has also joined the ranks of those physicians who believe that faith is an important ingredient in healing. He described his faith in a recent book, *Beyond the Relaxation Response* (Times Books, 1984), and he was interviewed for the May 1984 issue of *American Health*. Benson stated that medicine can help only 25% of those coming to doctor's offices for treatment. He advocated prayer and meditation to release the powerful effects of faith.

And in the same issue of *American Health* is an article, "Healers in Mainstream," that tells of the cardiologist William Haynes, who is praying for his patients by using the laying-on-of-hands. He was surprised to find that medical students and interns often ask for help to form prayer groups. There is, in fact, a Christian Medical Foundation with about 2000 like-minded physicians as members. In Baltimore, Dr. Kenneth Bakken is one of the founders of St. Luke's Health Ministries; among other things, this group operates a clinic in a Lutheran church where both medical and sacramental healing are offered. Bakken recently published a book, *The Call to Wholeness* (Crossroad), in which he described this effective joining of two ministries.

When we understand the impact that faith can have upon our emotions and bodies, we realize that an experience of God plays a creative role in both physical and psychological healing. Real prayer, which gives us an experience of the purpose and meaning in the universe, as well as a real knowledge of and relationship with God, can have incredible, observable healing power. Seldom does illusion have this kind of repeatable effect.

4

MANY WORLDS OF EXPERIENCE AND WAYS OF KNOWING THEM

How, then, can we know that there is meaning in the universe? How do we receive information from a world beyond our physical selves? At one period in his life, Aldous Huxley ingested a considerable quantity of mescalin. He then did what most people who take drugs do not do: he reflected on his experience and wrote a book, *Doors of Perception.* In it he offered the most adequate understanding in recent Western thinking about how we know the world around us. Huxley agreed with Dr. C. D. Board who said:

> We should do well to consider much more carefully than we have hitherto been inclined to do the type of theory which Bergson put forward in connection with memory and sense perception. The suggestion is that the function of the brain and nervous system and sense organs is in the main *eliminative* and not productive. Each person is at each moment capable of remembering all that has ever happened to him and of perceiving everything that is happening everywhere in the universe. The function of the brain and nervous system is to protect us from being overwhelmed and confused by this mass of largely useless and

irrelevant knowledge, by shutting out most of what we should otherwise perceive or remember at any moment, and leaving only that very small and special selection which is likely to be practically useful.[1]

Huxley went on to suggest that the enormous quantity of information that human beings can receive is funneled through the reduction valve of the brain and nervous system. "What comes out at the other end," he said, "is a measly trickle of the kind of consciousness which will help us to stay alive on the surface of this particular planet."

He went on to point out that the problem is compounded as we express this reduced awareness in "those symbol-systems and implicit philosophies which we call language." Languages are both a great help and a hindrance: they are a help in that they can give us the stored-up written knowledge of other people's experience; they are a hindrance in that they make us victims of a one-sided view of reality, confirming us in the idea that this reduced awareness is the *only experience to be had.* In our Western world we have lived so long within a materialistic framework that we have only one word to express contact with other than material reality—the word *mysticism.* And that word has a bad press. Furthermore, what is often, in a derogatory way, called "this world"—in the language of religion, for example—is what Huxley called "the universe of reduced awareness, expressed and, as it were, petrified by language. The various 'other worlds' with which human beings erratically make contact are so many elements in the totality of the awareness . . . ," what Huxley called "Mind at Large." Huxley continued:

> Most people, most of the time, know only what comes through the reducing valve and is consecrated as genuinely real by the local language. Certain persons, however, seem to be born with a kind of by-pass that circumvents the reducing valve. In others temporary by-passes may be acquired either spontaneously, or

as the result of deliberate "spiritual exercises," or through hypnosis, or by means of drugs. Through these permanent or temporary by-passes there flows, not indeed the perception "of everything that is happening everywhere in the universe" (for the by-pass does not abolish the reducing valve, which still excludes the total content of Mind at Large) but something more than, and above all something different from, the carefully selected utilitarian material which our narrowed, individual minds regard as a complete, or at least sufficient, picture of reality.

Prayer, meditation, religious practices, and rituals can open us to just such another dimension of existence in which there is a saving reality, a reality we Christians find essentially and totally embodied in the person of Jesus of Nazareth, living, crucified, and resurrected. A student at Notre Dame in a class on the phenomenology of religious experience asked me the following question: "Why has no one in my 16 years of religious education ever explained to me that I could obtain experiences of another dimension through prayer and meditation better than I could through the use of drugs?" Unless we have a theory of how we can know "other worlds," we seldom can offer a way to experience them.

In *The Psychology of Consciousness* (Penguin, 1973), Robert Ornstein, a research psychologist at Langley Porter Neuropsychiatric Institute and a teacher at the University of California Medical Center, espoused a view of human knowing that is based on this passage from Huxley's book, as well as on the thinking of C. D. Broad and Henri Bergson; Ornstein used Huxley's theory to understand the important differences between the right and left sides of the brain. Furthermore, one of the most perceptive thinkers in epistemology (the philosophical study of how we know) was Arthur O. Lovejoy, of Johns Hopkins University, and he came to similar conclusions. He concluded his book *The Revolt Against Dualism* (Open Court, 1960) by stating that he could not really understand how we can know and that the best he could do was end with a myth—as Plato did. Lovejoy's myth tells of creation; when God created the world, Lovejoy suggested, he made only *things,* but then he realized that something was missing. So he created *knowing* to fill the gap, and he added it to creation. And this *knowing* was the germ from which our consciousness developed.

One of the most dramatic evidences I have seen of this theory is the film *The Embattled Cell,* available through the American Cancer Society. It is a 3000-magnification time-lapse movie of living lung tissue infected with cancer cells. Lymphocytes, one-celled organisms with no sense organs, try to enter cancer cells in an apparently purposeful way. Clusters of cancer cells die an explosive death after several lymphocytes have entered them.

Although Jung never developed such a clear theory—or myth—of how we know, his works are filled with the results of using this kind of knowing. The same can be said of William James. All of these thinkers awaken us to the fact that we cannot deal with the whole reality of human beings until we cease limiting our knowledge to those data that can be received through the five senses alone.

Those of us who are caught in the materialistic Western world view, and yet have experienced the spiritual world described by Christianity, may find it easier to believe that this spiritual reality can have an effect on our *minds* than that it can touch our bodies. In fact, though, such an idea is logically flawed; for a consistent materialist, all our knowledge is passed to us through our five senses—through our bodies, in other words. According to such a view, if we were to receive a message from outside the materialistic box, something would have to come and move the cogs of our physical organism. But is this the way Scripture says that knowledge comes to us? The Bible does not state that we receive all our knowledge through the five senses. We have picked up that idea from our culture and assumed that it reflects the biblical viewpoint. In fact, though, the materialistic view jibes with neither Scripture nor modern science. For many people in our time, it is easier to believe in the reports of those who describe an experience of God's saving love when we realize that there is increasing evidence in scientific circles that we humans are not limited to experience received through the five senses. Psychological theories that do not deal with the reality of both sensory and nonsensory experience are not dealing with the actual world in which we live or with all the possibilities of knowing that are open to human beings.

Other Evidence

Mircea Eliade is one of the most important students of comparative religion today. His book *Shamanism* (Princeton, 1964) is the authoritative and definitive study of the religious view that maintains that human beings can be in touch with the spiritual world.

And Eliade is at present editing *The Encyclopedia of Religion*. He takes seriously human contact with a spiritual dimension of reality. (Hastings' *Encyclopedia of Religion and Ethics*, published in this century's rationalistic early years, equates miracles with magic.) Most of the writers in the early church similarly never doubted that the gods of the pagans were real, but they considered them only a partial aspect of spiritual reality and not its essence, its heart. Evil rears its head whenever a partial aspect of reality, especially an inferior part, pretends to be the whole. Therefore we fall into evil whenever we worship anything that exists in the spiritual domain that is less than God most fully revealed in Jesus Christ, the God characterized by the ultimate power in all reality—self-giving, transforming love.

Interesting work is being done in the School of World Mission at Fuller Seminary by Dr. Peter Wagner and his associates. They are trying to prepare students for mission work by opening them to the reality of a spiritual or psychoid dimension of experience. They have discovered that people of Third World countries are better acquainted with this dimension than most Westerners. Dr. Wagner referred me to an article by Dr. Paul Hiebert (also of that school) entitled "The Flaw of the Excluded Middle."[2] Hiebert argued that Western rationalistic materialism has eliminated our knowledge of principalities and powers, of the angelic and demonic, and left us with an ideal world of spirit that we know only by revelation and not by experience *and* the material reality known by sense data; there is nothing between these. Dr. Wagner told me that in trying to bring the Christian message to people of a different culture, Western missionaries often transmit the message of secularism rather than the message of a saving, transforming Christ; in so doing, they actually contribute to the secularization of the people of these societies. Missionaries need a wider world view if they are to present the message of Christ to the people Jung saw as still having a healthy view of reality.

In four studies of Germany's Nazi catastrophe published in *Civilization in Transition* (Princeton, 1970), Jung pointed out that Nazism was actually an inferior religious movement. The god they worshiped was Wotan, a brutal god of war. Jung said that one could have predicted that the movement would collapse just as the world of these Germanic gods was destroyed in the final myth portrayed in Wagner's operas. And in a new book called *Unmasking the Powers* (Fortress, 1986), Walter Wink has analyzed the New Testament passages on the principalities and powers, and reminds us that unless we deal with them in Christ, these forces will deal with us. The spiritual world and its potent powers are real, as Jesus reminds us again and again.

Although hallucinogenic drug use gets less public attention than it used to, the latest statistics show that nearly two-thirds of all young adults occasionally use marijuana and that one-third use one of the more powerful drugs. So anyone working with young people from the early teens through the twenties needs to understand drug use if they are going to deal with this age group effectively. The best study of the problem is probably by Andrew Weil, a Harvard M.D., who has worked with the government in drug control. His book *The Natural Mind: A New Way of Looking at Drugs and the Higher Consciousness* (Houghton Mifflin, 1972) maintains that the main reason young people use hallucinogenic drugs is to break out of the materialistic world view of their parents; he contends that there is an instinctual desire in people to deal with more than the material world. My experience in college teaching bears out the 1982 government statistics as well as Weil's thesis. For many young people today, drug use is a dangerous form of "pop" meditation.

Alcoholics Anonymous is the most successful treatment program for one of the most tragic forms of addiction. The essence of its method is the individual's surrender to a *real power* beyond the human being. Teen Challenge has had remarkable success with hard drug users; the heart of rehabilitation for this group consists of bringing addicted teenagers to a relationship with and reliance upon the resurrected Christ. Similarly, David Wilkerson's *The Cross and the Switchblade* (Revell) describes the transforming power found in the Pentecostal experience— a direct experience of the Holy Spirit. When people experience the reality of God's saving grace, they are much less susceptible to inferior forms of transpersonal experience.

With all the evidence of the effect and power of religious experience in enabling people to overcome their psychological and addiction problems as well as their physical ones, it is amazing how little interest is shown in this area by health

professionals. A recent survey of the religious attitudes of social workers, therapists, psychologists, psychiatrists, and pastoral counselors by Dr. Timothy Kochems for his doctoral
dissertation at George Washington University showed that most
of these professionals are uncomfortable when religious material is presented by their clients. Seldom will these ''helpers''
actually initiate questions pertaining to religion. The use of
religion or religious practices for overt psychological purposes
is generally discouraged in the health field. The less religious
these therapists are in their own experiential beliefs and practices, the less likely they are to view others' religious partic-
ipation in a positive way. Indeed, those with little acquaintance
with experiential religion often have a negative attitude toward
religion, both emotionally and theoretically.

Dr. J. Andrew Canale, a psychologist working in the Boston
area who has written several books on psychological and religious subjects, is working on a study showing that practically
no major modern therapists have focused on the importance of
religious faith in the treatment of depression, even though the
loss of meaning is one of the most significant ingredients in
the majority of depressive conditions.[3]

When we take even a cursory look at the data emerging from
physics, mathematics, religion, sociology, parapsychology,
and biology, as well as psychology, it becomes quite evident
that it takes *faith* to uphold the *materialistic* view of our universe. The shoe is actually on the other foot; it takes even more
faith to maintain that we are nothing but atoms or genes than
it does to believe that we are part of a complex and mysterious
universe that is partly physical and partly spiritual. A loving
''Abba'' is always reaching out to us, and he even came among
us in Jesus of Nazareth to complete creation and offer salvation
to human beings. ''But God demonstrates his own love for us
in this: While we were still sinners, Christ died for us. . . .
how much more, having been reconciled, shall we be saved

through his life!'' (Rom. 5:8,10). So for us who would bring healing to a world still imprisoned in a materialistic world view it is important to know its philosophical flaws and to realize that its faith is less historical, less substantial, than our own.

The Gifts of the Spirit

Paul's most careful statement concerning the gifts of the Spirit is found in 1 Corinthians 12:6—14:40. These gifts can be grouped together in six categories:

1. gifts of healing and miracles;
2. gifts of revelation—dreams, visions, intuitions; these are experiences of the other side and of those who dwell in it, including God, Christ, the faithful departed (the communion of saints), and also the demonic;
3. gifts of discernment, through which we discern whether the angelic or demonic is operating in any dimension of reality, including human lives;
4. gifts of wisdom and knowledge, by which we obtain information that is inaccessible to reason and sense experience;
5. gifts of proclamation: prophecy, tongue speaking, and the interpretation of tongues;
6. the gift of love, which expresses the essence of the risen Christ and enables us to live within the Holy Spirit and use all its gifts creatively.

Some time ago I realized that Christian theology has had little to say about these gifts. Many liberals simply dismiss them as a superstitious addition to the pure ethical milk of the gospel. At the same time, some conservatives maintain that these gifts—though real—were granted by dispensation only in biblical times to get the church started, and then they were withdrawn. Both the conservatives and the liberals are denying the present reality of the gifts for the same reason; they both have accepted the basic materialistic view of the universe, and they are trying to adjust their Christian faith and practice to that view.

In the New Testament the gifts of the spirit (the *charismata*) are considered the observable evidence of spiritual activity within the space-time world. But if we are indeed imprisoned in a purely materialistic universe, the gifts must be either an illusion, a delusion, or a special dispensation granted by God. Rudolf Bultmann clearly adopted this thesis in his article on demythologizing, in which he flatly called "mythological" any statement claiming that a reality which is not physical is operating in the space-time world. Bultmann also thought that this secular age would not accept the gospel as long as it was expressed in such "mythological" language. From such a viewpoint the idea that God or a spiritual dimension of reality can have a healing effect on our psychological lives would also have to be categorized as myth.

A friend and collaborator, Paisley Roach, and I once read through the entire New Testament looking for evidence of these gifts. We marked with colored crayon all verses "contaminated" with the first five of these intrusions of the spiritual world into our own. It was only then that we truly realized that love without a divine dimension is not the love that Jesus was talking about. We discovered that no less than 3,874 verses of the 7,957 of the New Testament were "contaminated" with one or more the first five of these spiritual gifts.[4] People trapped within a materialistic world view cannot comprehend 49% of these biblical passages, so they delete or ignore them or say they apply only to another time. To make the magnitude of these deletions more apparent and dramatic, Roach took a razor and cut out the marked passages, producing a mutilated book I called *The Gospel According to Rational Materialism*.

Then I tried to find adequate studies of these gifts in modern theological writing. There was little to be found—almost nothing written in a careful, scholarly, critical manner. I have, in fact, spent much of the last 20 years dealing with one after the other of the gifts. First I wrote on the subject of tongue speaking. I then turned my attention to the gift of revelation and wrote on prayer as revelation; over the years I have written several books on this central subject. Then I dealt with the subject of healing, which had interested me from the time I came to know Agnes Sanford and her writings. Then I dealt with the gift of wisdom and knowledge, after which I turned to the subject of discernment and produced a study of it. The subject of Christian love also demanded a careful study. One of my most notable observations during these years was of the development of a course on "Signs and Wonders" at Fuller Seminary (reported in the October 1982 issue of *Christian Life*). Some branches of conservative and orthodox Christianity seem, at last, to be breaking out of the shackles of materialistic dispensationalism; they have discovered that the "demythologized" gospel is difficult to present in the missionary context.

When the New Testament is seen as either full of holes or applying only to a time gone by, it is little wonder that many people have felt that they are not nourished in Christian churches and have turned either to authoritarian sects or to Eastern religions for nourishment.

Far from being critical of Rudolf Bultmann, the leading proponent of demythologized Christianity, I am deeply grateful that he had the courage to point out the implications of materialism for the Christian gospel. Most of Bultmann's actual contributions to biblical criticism, by the way, are quite independent of this theological framework.

Let us turn now to the Christian drama of salvation and see how each part of it can have a healing effect upon our souls, minds, and bodies. And I doubt if we can be whole in the latter two aspects of our being if we are not healed in soul.

5

CHRISTIANITY

AS HEALING LOVE AND HOPE

The resurrection of Jesus has been the foundation of my faith for many years. As I tried to explain what the resurrection meant to me, I found that I could not adequately deal with this mystery until I put it in the context of the entire Christian drama of salvation. I began to see that the resurrection was crucial because a specific person, Jesus of Nazareth, was raised from the dead. This event affirmed and ratified Jesus' life, as well as his teachings, healings, love, and courageous death. The resurrection did not have cosmic significance for me until I understood that this human being was not an ordinary person. Jesus was the self-emptying God entering our world in the flesh, through his incarnation. And God entered our world because evil had corrupted us; only if God confronted evil could we be delivered from it.

I continued to reflect on what happened after the resurrection: this glorified person ascended back to God. So what had happened *did* have cosmic significance. And to give us struggling people continual encouragement and power, the Holy Spirit—the spirit of Jesus and God—was poured out upon all who would receive it. The last part of the drama, however, depends on us. We need to respond to this outpouring of love and to share with others what has been given to us. To quote the words of Irenaeus, "Jesus became what we are in order that we might become what he is."

Equipped by this understanding, I have imagined Christianity as a seven-act drama or an arch of seven stones. Each of the acts of the play is essential to the action, just as each stone is necessary if the arch is to stand. Let us look at the different parts of the drama; then we will go on to see the psychological significance and importance of each of them, since the divine drama deals with every human need.

Act 1.   God creates the world and it is good; the Logos stretches out the heavens and the earth, the physical world and the vast spiritual dimension of reality. God creates because God loves. However, some of the created angelic hosts come to think that they are equal to God; they rebel, putting power in place of love. Human society is corrupted by these powers.

Act 2.   Creation continues in the incarnation of Jesus. God knows our human plight and, out of infinite love, comes into this world to rescue human beings and to give them the opportunity of coming to him: God, in Christ, puts aside divinity and becomes one of us. (Self-effacing love is real, and it is the very nature of God.)

Act 3.   God reveals to humankind Jesus Christ's divine nature *within the world* by living as an ordinary baby, child, and adolescent. As an adult, Jesus sets out to preach, teach, and heal, to reveal the precise nature of God, the self-giving, unbounded love that is God's nature—that is, indeed, the meaning undergirding all reality. Then Jesus courageously meets evil on the cross and submits to it, making clear for us the way that we need to follow.

Act 4.   In the resurrection, the way of love and nonviolence is victoriously affirmed. Jesus rises from the dead and evil is defeated. He appears to the disciples, who have denied him and let him down; they are transformed and become victorious as well.

Act 5.   In the ascension, Jesus as a divine-human being resumes his eternal cosmic place and now becomes available to all people in all times and places.

Act 6.   At Pentecost the risen and cosmic Christ sends the Spirit in a new way upon all who will receive it. A new era opens for human beings.

Act 7.   But the divine drama is not complete until we respond to the limitless divine love, mercy, and healing power revealed in these previous six acts; it is not complete until we humans allow the cosmic victory to be an earthly and human one in us.[1]

Obviously one could write a good-sized book about each of these aspects of the Christian drama of redemption. And another book could be written about the psychological implications of each of these different parts of Christianity—what they tell us about our human nature and how we need to treat one another if we wish to be healing agents of God for those around us. However, my purpose here is merely to suggest some of the psychological meanings embedded in the total Christian story, to show that Jesus and the Christian faith in him, understood in depth, provide a profound and adequate psychology of human beings.

God knew the psychological truth that human beings are more touched by stories than by logical propositions, so he gave us this divine story, this divine drama played out upon the stage of history. Helen Luke has drawn my attention to the magnificent statement of Harold Goddard: "The destiny of the world is determined less by the battles that are lost and won than by the stories it loves and believes in."[2] God, therefore, provided a divine story for us to believe in and shape our lives around.

Act 1: Creation and the Problem of Evil

The most poignant problem for Christians is why there is evil in God's good creation. We look out into the world and see sickness, bloodshed, war, racial tension, concentration camps, discrimination against women and racial minorities and all those who differ from the social norm, prejudice, poverty, human agony, and a foul prison system. When we look within our own souls or listen to friends and others who come to us for support, we often see self-destructive behavior, arrogance, despair, anguish, pain, bereavement, defeat, brokenness, mental illness, and suicidal darkness. What is wrong?

Neither Jesus nor vital Christianity has ever tried to whitewash the world and pretend that it is pleasant for all, nor do they try to maintain that these ugly parts of life are unreal. In his ministry Jesus fought against the manifestations of the Evil One in sickness, mental illness, the myriad forms of moral corruption, and even death itself. In Revelation 12:7-9 we are told that there was war in heaven and that Satan was cast out of heaven onto the earth. Satan and his hosts of fallen angels have turned against the God of love, and in their loneliness and separation they try to drag fragile humanity with them into rebellion.

Sometimes it seems as though we struggle directly with the "cosmic powers and principalities who are the source of the darkness of this world, the spiritual hosts of evil in the heavens" (Eph. 6:12, auth. trans.). Then we realize that the often painful picture of the human condition presented in the New Testament is wholly realistic. When I began to study the depth of my own inner being with some of Jung's followers, I began for the first time truly to understand the meaning of the term *original sin*. This "sin" is the collective inheritance of generations of fallen, broken people; such brokenness wears thin the walls of our souls and makes us more vulnerable to the direct incursions of the dark reality that is so clearly among us.

When I come to feel my own inner darkness, it is extremely helpful to know that I am not alone, that I share in a common human fate. Some years ago, as I was wrestling with this inner darkness, I remember going around a bend in the Pasadena freeway and suddenly realizing that all other human beings were nearly as mixed up as I. I understood Paul's words: "The whole creation has been groaning as in the pains of childbirth right up to the present time" (Rom. 8:22). When we have experienced this inner helplessness, we can share with others in their agony. When we can admit to those who are suffering that we have experienced similar pain, we open up real communication with them.

Those who are suffering are often afraid that anyone who knew what they are like inside would reject them. When we let them know, therefore, that we have experienced the same kind of helplessness and self-recrimination as they, the first bridge is built to sharing, to caring, to becoming instruments of healing. Often when people have gathered up their courage to come to see me in my office and are fearful that they will not be heard or accepted, I tell them that I do not look down my long and bony nose at people as if they were specimens; rather, I reach out a hand to them as if they were brothers or sisters struggling with the same kinds of problems I have had. I agree with Unamuno, who said that the chief sanctity of a temple is that humans can go there to weep together. Self-disclosure is encouraged by this attitude; there can be little psychological help given until another is free to share with us.

It would be terrible if I were still under the law and there was no redemption. A deeply prayerful Christian friend of mine was once speaking to a Jewish rabbi from the mystical tradition.

As they were sharing, the rabbi asked, "But aren't you frightened when you find yourself in the awesome presence of God?" My monastic friend replied, "No, this is what Christ's love does for me." Without this love, only the truly heroic could dare to enter God's presence, knowing the darkness and evil they carry.

The realization that by myself I cannot deal with these dark forces that surround me, that I am helpless, represents precisely the kind of surrender to which we referred earlier. Paul reminded us that if we allow it, the Spirit will come to aid us in our weakness. But life is ghastly if I face this anxiety alone, with no hope. Then I fall into the well of darkness, which Camus and Sartre described so despairingly. A great gulf separates those who face anxiety without hope and those who have found the aid of the Spirit. Those who face this inner evil with no hope or light often find themselves in the grip of serious depression.

Acknowledging that of and by ourselves we are helpless can give us humility. This allows us to look generously at others who are broken without moralizing. We step into their misery with them (after all, there but for the grace of God go I). Out of this shared suffering empathy grows, authentic empathy, the beginning of any truly healing relationship. This empathy can give us the confidence we need to remember that the Christian community is not a museum for saints but a hospital for sinners, that the waves of darkness continue to beat against our shores and to touch even the most holy. All of us cry out with Paul, "Who will rescue me from this body of death?" (Rom. 7:24).

Acknowledging our helplessness, our brokenness, our "caughtness" in the evils of the world, our sinfulness—this is the beginning of true religion and holiness. The greatest of the saints, like Francis of Assisi or Teresa of Avila, often maintained that they were the worst of sinners. Those who have approached nearest to the holiness of God are most aware of their faults and inadequacies. When we reflect in depth, we realize that all of us fall short of living up to the beatitudes or to the example of Jesus of Nazareth.

For therapists in either the secular or religious setting, acknowledging brokenness and inadequacy is the first step to becoming healers. Most effective healers are wounded healers. Speaking to a group of clergy, Jung said, "We cannot change anything unless we accept it. Condemnation does not liberate; it oppresses. I am the oppressor of the person that I condemn, not his friend and fellow sufferer." He went on to say that it is impossible not to condemn and judge unless we see and accept ourselves as we are. He described how most of us avoid our own darkness and concluded: "The man who uses modern psychology to look behind the scenes not only of his patients' lives but more especially of his own—and the modern psychotherapist must do this if he is not to be merely an unconscious fraud—will admit that to accept himself in all his wretchedness is the hardest of tasks, and one which it is almost impossible to fulfill."[3] Jesus' repeated injunction, "Do not judge, or you too will be judged," or his statement, "If any one of you is without sin, let him be the first to throw a stone at her," remind us that this attitude is equally important for religion and psychotherapy.

We need not despair. The next act of our cosmic drama provides a better answer to our lostness than we could have hoped for.

Act 2: God in Flesh Among Us

God comes among us as one of us. God knew that messages from prophets were not enough; human beings need God's own presence, touch, and forgiving love. How did God come? As a bolt of lightning, or as a blazing manifestation of power? No. In Christ God put aside power and divinity and humbly became incarnate in a woman—and the place of women began to change in a world in which men had formerly treated them as inferiors. Christ was born in a stable, a Middle Eastern stable, with oxen and sheep. There was no place for him in palaces, in the humblest peasant's home, or even in an inn for weary travelers. Christ was born of humble villagers in an occupied country. Why? So that none of us could say that God did not know and come down to our lowly place.

Raymond Brown has provided an excellent scholarly analysis of the stories about the birth of Jesus in his book *The Birth of the Messiah* (Doubleday, 1977). His conclusion is much the same as mine; there are few places in the entire gospel story where the essence of Christian theology is presented with greater clarity and insight than in the birth narratives.[4]

What love and humility this birth reveals! Kierkegaard likened the birth narrative of Jesus to the story of a great emperor who loved his people, but found he could not come close to them until he put on a disguise and came among them as the least of them. True humility and love are nearly always linked together. Paul reminds us in Philippians that we should take upon ourselves the mind of Christ: "Who, being in very nature God, did not consider equality with God something to be grasped, but made himself nothing, taking the very nature of a servant [slave], being made in human likeness. And being found in appearance as a man, he humbled himself and became obedient to death—even death on a cross!" (2:6-8).

As we face our own darkness, we know the humility of equal burdens; but when we understand God's coming in the flesh, we know that we also share equal worth. It is ennobling, but also humbling, to know that God in Christ wishes to be our brother: for most of us it is more difficult to accept our eternal value than it is to acknowledge our human helplessness.

The story of Christmas is the story of love humbly poured

so it would not intimidate. Deep in each of our hearts there is a longing for that love. Even if tragedy and pain and cruelty have nearly quenched that longing, it still remains. For a moment at Christmas we are fired by this image, touched by its truth, which rings on Christmas Day like a bell that has long been unsounded. In Jesus' birth God came not to judge human beings, but with humble, seeking love to meet their longing and need. In dealing with others the best method to follow is that of Jesus—patient, humble love. Judging others seldom heals other people. Most people are already judging themselves too harshly. They need to know through us God's infinite love. God made us restless that we might find rest in divine love.

Christians who would reach out to other human beings to share healing and renewal will do so not just at Christmas time. Throughout the year they will try to live this humility and self-effacing love. That is authenticity. Such Christians, furthermore, will consider no person to be inferior. Those who carry the spirit of true Christianity will exemplify as much as possible the mind of Christ, and this will be equally true of Christian lay people, ministers, and therapists. Any therapist, in fact, who has this attitude will be building on the foundation laid by Christ, whether or not he or she acknowledges it. I seriously doubt that there is any other adequate way of treating human beings than the one Jesus reveals. As we truly face the evil in the world, we realize that humble caring is the most effective way to deal with human beings—and is the way, indeed, to touch the essential, loving nature of the universe.

Several of my psychologist friends have noted the increased crises in their patients at Christmas time. One of them called it "the Christmas neurosis." As Christmas comes, these patients expect to find the same concern and love and caring that they experienced as children at Christmas. When they do not find it, darkness invades them with its mocking voice.

Few people in history have better embodied the nature of God revealed in the incarnation than Francis of Assisi. Few statements embody that life better than the prayer attributed to him. Whether or not he wrote it is inconsequential; it was his prayer because he lived it. It provides a method for all who would be healers:

> Lord, make me an instrument of your peace; where there is hatred, let me sow love; where there is injury, pardon; where there is doubt, faith; where there is despair, hope; where there is darkness, light; where there is weakness, strength; and where there is sadness, joy.
>
> O Divine Master, grant that I may not so much seek to be consoled as to console; to be understood as to understand; to be loved as to love; for it is in giving that we receive, it is in pardoning that we are pardoned, and it is in dying that we are born to eternal life.

However, we cannot love consistently and act with continuous humility until we realize that this requires an effort on our part. One of the major paradoxes in Christianity is this: I cannot help myself by my own effort alone, and yet God's transforming love will not be operative in me unless I cooperate with it. I need, therefore, grace *and* discipline. In his book *The Road Less Traveled* (Simon and Schuster, 1980) the psychiatrist M. Scott Peck pointed out that none of us can truly love until we learn the importance of discipline and seek to gain some control over our desires and emotions. We need to deal with our craving for power; our egocentricity, anger, and hatred; our thirst for vengeance; our jealousy; our sexual feelings; and our fear, laziness, and hopelessness.

I find it relatively easy to be totally accepting, caring, and humble for an hour with nearly any human being in my office. It is far more difficult, however, to achieve this with my family, with whom I have lived for 24 hours a day. And yet there is something unreal and inauthentic in what I do in my office if the same attitude I have there does not carry over to my family, to those with whom I work, to those whom I meet casually, to the strangers drifting off alone into the shadows—even to the enemy.

One of the main reasons that people come to therapists is that they know few other places where they can find the concern and listening that so many people are starving for. But the art of listening is something that all Christians need to nurture. God, in Christ, came among us as the humblest of human beings so that we would not be overawed and could freely speak of our brokenness and fears and be listened to. In the congregation where I was pastor, we were frequently reminded by Ollie Backus that people are not truly loving until they have learned to listen to one another. And yet how few churches provide this first step to love, training in listening, for their congregation. And sometimes we don't even find listening in psychologists' offices, in spite of the statement of Bruno Klopfer, the authority on the Rorschach test, that 50% of all effective psychotherapy is warm, understanding listening. It is possible *to learn* to listen.

Jung pointed out how Christianity brought a new attitude into the world. Jesus' coming into the world provided a goal for human beings to follow: he called on us to begin to take responsibility for our lives and control our outbursts of anger, judgment, and hatred. The emphasis Jesus placed on love forced us to discipline ourselves, and this brought a new level of consciousness and self-awareness into human society. The more we know about ourselves, the less happy we are with our strides toward this goal. We fail again and again, and yet we try not to become discouraged. (Indeed, discouragement is usually only disillusioned egotism.)

However, when discipline is not directed toward love and with love, it can become demonic. When all of our instinctual nature is suppressed or repressed, the result can be psychological illness. When the body and its natural appetites are rejected as evil, we become less than human. Unfortunately, some Christian groups have taken this approach, and their more sensitive members have had to suffer or seek psychological help. God made the body, and it was good. Jesus lived as a human being among human beings, laughing, crying, enjoying his friends, going to dinner parties. God made us partly spirit and partly beast. Our task is not to grind out either part, but to use *discipline* to bring these two parts into harmony. This task is a difficult one, and we fail again and again. We need to continue to return again and again to hear the psychological message of the next two acts in the Christian epic.

Act 3: The Image of God in a Human Being

The birth of Christ is important, but if Herod had accomplished his goal and killed the infant Jesus, we would have only the skeleton of the Christian faith. If we want to follow God and be in harmony with the divine way, we have to know what God is like. The incarnation tells us that God is like Jesus of Nazareth; Jesus' life and teachings give us a clear picture of what it is like to live God's reality in this actual world. Jesus preached, taught, healed, and died.

According to Mark, Jesus began his ministry by proclaiming to the crowds that followed him that the kingdom of heaven, the reign of God, was at hand, available now. He announced that what we hope to know fully in the resurrected life in the kingdom beyond this dimension of reality can be touched and participated in in the present, human world. The broken, the sick, the defeated, the guilty, the anxious, and the poor heard Jesus and were changed by his words of authority. Few, however, of the complacent, the rich, or the self-satisfied followed him. Jesus' basic message was, whoever you are or whatever you may have been, God wants to receive you and give you life abundantly both now and forever. The task of true therapy is the same: to reach out to the suffering and to bring them the kind of abundant life that can lead to the joy of eternal life.

From the beginning of Jesus' ministry, one of his central tasks was to heal the sick of body, mind, and soul. Jean Leclercq, the eminent Benedictine medieval scholar, pointed out that there is no better evidence of the love of God than the healing ministry of Jesus. Jesus touched the blind, the lame, and the dead, and they were healed; he rebuked the forces that brought mental illness and demonic possession, and human beings were freed from them.

Can we truly be Christians if we too are not concerned about the sickness of others? If we are followers of Christ, we will minister to the suffering of others with whatever gifts we have. They may be gifts of service (a hot meal, for example), of medicine, of caring and listening, of psychological therapy, of the laying-on-of-hands, or of financial help. As we try to imitate Christ, therefore, it is important not to force our lives slavishly into the pattern of Jesus' particular activities, but to allow the Spirit to guide us to live our lives according to our own special gifts. Particularly for young adults, being open to understanding all the various facets of their emerging selves is an important step in discerning how and why the Spirit is calling. Only in this way will we integrate the essence of Jesus' loving life into our own life patterns.

Jesus taught, and his first message echoed the meaning of the incarnation itself. All human beings, he revealed, have an infinite value before God, and no one person can be sacrificed for another. Jews, Greeks, barbarians, men, women, slaves, blacks, whites, drug users, alcoholics, and the morally depraved are infinitely valuable to God. If we wish to follow God's way, we are never to condemn another; as Jesus said, "Do not judge, or you too will be judged." Only this attitude can help us to forgive others, and Jesus knew the psychological truth that it is our forgiveness, not our condemnation, that leads others to wholeness. When we deal with hurting people in nonjudgmental acceptance, we begin to be agents of God's healing love. This does not mean that we should avoid pointing out that certain paths can lead to disaster, but we must do this with humility and love rather than with self-righteous arrogance. Only when we are humble, can we begin to listen, and not judge. Then we are able to forgive and to be ministers of God's own forgiveness. Our human love can then be sacramentalized and become a carrier of the God who is love.

The story of the prodigal son is really the story of the prodigal father—God. The father treats both the returned profligate younger brother and the arrogant, scornful, workaholic elder brother with the same warmth and compassion and love. One reason that it is so hard to believe this story or what it says about God is that so few of us have ever been treated this way.

Better than anyone else, Jesus taught us the value of women and children, and so of families. The family unit was for Jesus holy and sacred, and Jesus assumed that we would try to love those who love us. Jesus also defied the patriarchal Jewish attitude in the law on divorce. Women had equal value with men and could not just be discarded. In addition, Jesus appeared first to Mary Magdalene, as Walter Wink has pointed out, and so again emphasized the value of women.[5] However, the institutional church could not sustain so radical a view and dropped this account out of later versions of the resurrection. Paul Davies, the physicist to whom we referred earlier, wrote that the status of women in many religious groups, Christianity included, made him wonder about the morality of ''religion.''

When women and children are valued, then sexuality is sanctified. God made it to give joy to human beings and to perpetuate the species. Sexuality can be holy. There are some who find that a sexual life is not right for them, that it impedes their religious journey, but such people are the exceptions rather than the rule. It is true that in the early days of Christianity many believers took the vow of celibacy. This was not because there was anything morally wrong with marriage and sexuality, but because they thought that only within a celibate life could they be free to follow Christ's way. One of the grievances that fueled the progress of the Reformation was the rule of required celibacy for all clergy and the implication this practice had for the value of human sexuality.

Jesus retired alone into the mountains or the desert to have fellowship with "Abba" (a word close in meaning to our "daddy"). Being human, therefore, did not keep Jesus from having an immediate and personal contact with the Divine Lover. Nor does it keep the rest of us from having such contact. Indeed, if Jesus needed to keep in touch with Abba, how much more do we. And we have other ways of communicating than through the five senses. Jesus, for example, gave us the Lord's Prayer, a method of prayer that is really more than a prayer; it is a way of praying, of addressing God directly.

When human beings need this kind of fellowship and reassurance, psychologists who do not know that relationship with a living God is possible are shortchanging their clients. How ironic that I should have first learned in a psychologist's office that communication with God is possible. I came into the office looking terrible after awakening at 2:00 A.M. and being unable to sleep again. Max Zeller asked me if I knew why I couldn't sleep and then went on to tell me that God wanted to talk with me. I growled that I hadn't heard anything like that in seminary. He replied: "That is the way God got in touch with Samuel. Do you think God has changed?" Something did speak within me as I got up in the middle of the night and listened. And then I went back to bed and went to sleep.

Roy Fairchild described prayer as "paying full and fervent

attention to all of God we know—in Jesus Christ—with all of yourself that you know.'' Jesus knew and taught the depth and complexity of the human being, the many levels and layers of our being. He told us of the demonic, which can possess us at a level below our knowledge and will, which demonstrates that human beings are far more than just human consciousness. Paul also affirmed this truth when he told us that the things he did not want to do he found himself doing, and the things he wanted to do he was unable to do. The existence of this unconscious depth that Jesus knew about is one reason that we must not judge one another. I sometimes translate the words of Jesus' prayer ''Forgive us our unconsciousness, as we forgive the unconsciousness of others.'' Again I learned about this depth of myself not from seminary or modern theologians, but from depth psychology and my experience of analysis.

Jesus also provided us with religious ritual. He went regularly to the temple and the synagogue services, where the people glorified God, brought their hurts, sought forgiveness, and asked for blessings. If Jesus needed the fellowship of worship, how much more do we. He accepted the baptism of John, furthermore, and gave us Christian Baptism. And one of the last gifts he gave to his followers was to institute the sacramental meal of the Eucharist. They could continue eating this meal together and know that Christ was as much with them as he had been with them at that last meal before his death. Worship together in all of these ritualized ways is a psychological need as well as a religious one.

Jesus knew that we human beings need symbols if we are to live adequate lives. If we do not have adequate religious symbols, then we seize upon inadequate, even demonic, symbols, as Hitler did. In many places Jung has written wisely about the necessity of adequate symbols for adequate lives but particularly in his lecture entitled ''The Symbolic Life.''[6]

After their last supper together, Jesus went out to face condemnation, torture, and death. Of course, he could have slipped away over the hills, but he loved us human beings so much that he was willing to die to show that love. (As we have already noted, Paul reminded us that this action of love took place before we had even begun to turn to God.) Jesus, therefore, followed through the destiny of love to the bitter end. And just before he left them, he washed their feet and asked them to continue to wash one another's feet as a symbol of their humble, serving love toward one another. He told them that they were not truly his disciples unless they loved one another with the same kind of self-giving, unconditional, life-affirming love with which he had loved them.

We can learn much from some of the humanistic psychologists, who, in spite of their theological views, have lived out this kind of love toward their clients better than many of us Christians have in relation to our families, friends, enemies, fellow church members, and strangers. The humanists sometimes show more faith in love than we Christians who are allegedly following the loving way of Jesus. Sometimes Christians need to be reminded that their institutions do not always reflect the spirit of their divine master. Freud was highly—and justly—critical of the Viennese Christianity that he experienced. Professor Edward V. Stein has suggested in an article, "Freud and the Christian Faith," that Freud pointed up the flaws in our Christianity and can bring us back to a more authentic practice of the Christian way.[7] I would add that Freud in his criticisms was, in fact, acting more in the spirit and morality of Jesus than a large part of the church of his time.

The courage of Jesus awes me. He faced the worst that human beings could do and responded with love and forgiveness. On the cross he even faced the inner darkness of despair, which more than anything else tells us that he shared our humanity and finally came through to peace. Too many people fail in their Christian outreach and in their therapeutic healing because they do not have the courage to push forward into the unknown, trusting in the spirit of love, the Holy Spirit. Paul Tillich has written in depth on the subject of courage in his book *The Courage To Be* (Yale, 1952).

But if Jesus' death was the end of the Christian drama, as some Christians have suggested, we would be left in a totally meaningless world. We would be given no solid evidence that God's love has conquered the full onslaught of evil. We would be left with the sad news that the best of human beings died in agony on a cross, and that such tragedy is all that we can expect in this world; there may be a realm of love and transformation, but it cannot penetrate into the physical world. Such a story would tell those who have already been crushed by life that there is indeed no hope. For the skeptic, no evidence of love's ultimate centrality would be available; any belief in God's power over evil would be only conjecture. In 1 Corinthians 15, Paul wrote, "If only for this life we have hope in Christ, we are to be pitied more than all men."

The despair of those who have followed the life of Jesus and see it end on the cross is much worse than the despair of those who merely face the problem of evil and find it difficult to believe that a good God could have created a situation in which so much pain has emerged. How can anyone claim to have a solution for this kind of despair who does not have something better to offer than a story of the best of humans torn and bleeding, dying on a cross? The more desperate our agony and need, the more inadequate and cruel is the shallow optimism of most humanistic psychology. In the face of human anguish, of the despair of meaninglessness, of impending death, of the ravenous attack of evil, secular psychology has little to offer. Only the psychologist armed with something more can offer healing to the worst of human agony.[8]

6

CHRISTIANITY AS REDEEMING AND TRANSFORMING LOVE

The resurrection of Jesus was so important that soon the Jewish observance of the Sabbath was replaced by a celebration of the resurrection on the first day of every week. Every Sunday, therefore, is a little Easter. The world was turned upside down. Love was triumphant. The Evil One was defeated. There was hope: suffering did not end in annihilation but in transformation. Jesus' broken, defeated disciples were renewed and empowered, and they went out to spread the best of news: God's entrance into the world was not brought to naught. The self-effacing, self-giving love of God was victorious, and it expressed the nature of reality in its inmost being.

Act 4: The Resurrection of Jesus

The resurrection of Jesus was a real, historical event. I get annoyed with those Christians who are so taken in by materialism that they do not believe that what the Gospels describe is *objective* history. Was the experience of resurrection a visionary appearance or a physical one? Was the tomb indeed empty? Of course the tomb was empty, and only people who do not believe that the spiritual world is real will doubt that the visionary experience of the glorified Christ was a historical event. I believe that the risen Jesus appeared in both a physical and visionary way to his followers. When modern physicists do not balk at the notion that light is both a wave and a particle, why should we balk at the idea that the resurrected Jesus was both spiritual glory and physical reality (sometimes revealed in one way and sometimes in another)?

The New Testament and the early church are solid witnesses to the most important event of all history. A recent book by Pinchas Lapide, *The Resurrection of Jesus: A Jewish Perspective* (Augsburg, 1983), concluded that the historical evidence, the facts of history, cannot be denied: Jesus' resurrection is an historical fact, although Lapide maintained that this does not make Jesus the Messiah.[1] Peter, however, recognized Jesus' role as the anointed one before the resurrection, but this did not sink into the depth of him. It took the experience of Jesus' resurrection to bring the total Peter to total devotion and fidelity to Jesus as Lord and Messiah.

The psychological significance of Jesus' rising from death is so great that we can only hint at it in this survey.[2] The cross without the resurrection is the ultimate disaster, but in light of the resurrection it becomes the final victory. We human beings are more logical than we ordinarily think, and we are far more convinced—even conquered—by facts than by ideas. The factual nature of this event changes our view of the universe and how it is constituted. As we begin to see the significance of the risen Christ, we can affirm with James Russell Lowell:

> *Truth forever on the scaffold,*
> *Wrong forever on the throne—*
> *Yet that scaffold sways the future,*
> *And, behind the dim unknown,*
> *Standeth God within the shadow,*
> *Keeping watch above his own.*

Nearly every psychologist has described the disastrous effect of fear on the human mind and body. Much of our anger and hostility is a reaction to this fear of life, of meaninglessness, of the void, of condemnation, of evil itself. When that anxiety becomes intolerable and we can bear it no longer, then we may well give up and fall into the bottomless pit of depression. Those who believe that they live in a meaningless world can expect to be afraid, angry, and depressed. But when the meaning and reality of the resurrection of Jesus is fully internalized, we are freed from final and ultimate fear, from despair.

Psychology cannot provide meaning; it can only mediate meaning. But psychologists who avoid wrestling with the nature of meaning fail those in need. I am grateful that when I myself confronted despair, anxiety, darkness, and evil, I met and worked with Max Zeller, a Jew who had known the horrors of a German concentration camp and who knew that only an experience of God saved him. To be able to treat the ultimate source of our psychological confusion, chaos, and despair, psychologists need to *know* some reality that makes sense of all this pain. Then they need to be able to mediate that knowledge—personally, intellectually, and experientially. Jung and his followers gave me the hope that if I achieved the numinous experience (for me, that of the risen Jesus), I would be released from the curse of pathology. I am grateful also to Dorothy Sayers' radio plays on the life of Christ, *The Man Born to Be King* (David and Charles, 1983). Sayers' presentation of the resurrection of Jesus showed me that the appearances of Jesus to his disciples can be seen as history, a view that liberal biblical study has eroded.

The resurrection of Jesus gives us the hope that life has meaning; it spurs us to grasp our freedom courageously and to set forth on the way of love and God. I know of no other event in history that can touch us in whatever condition we find ourselves. How can psychology do its task if it ignores this reality? The resurrection tells us that God raises up what he loves. The life and message of Jesus tells us of God's unfailing, ever-seeking love for each of us. This points to a resurrected life for each of us after death, a life in which we can realize our infinite potential. We know that God's love will raise us up either at our death or at the second coming.

Act 5: The Incarnate Son of God Ascends

If Jesus had been raised, what happened to his body? Without the ascension, Jesus was more or less tied to one place and time. Although Jesus' resurrection appearances to his disciples gave some clues about his cosmic nature, only as he parted from them in a blaze of glory did they fully understand who this person was. That made this a parting without sorrow. In losing their master, they were more fully in touch with him than ever. David Stanley, a Jesuit and a student of Loyola's *Spiritual Exercises,* has written that after the ascension and Pentecost, Jesus became "more dynamically present in the world than ever he was when he walked the hills of Galilee."[3] As we turn back to these events in our imagination, we can be opened to the transforming power of the risen Lord and can be led "both to repeat in our own lives the redeeming experiences of Jesus' own existence and to participate personally in the paschal mystery."

In none of the early Christians' descriptions of the experience of Jesus' ascension is there expressed a sense of loss. Rather, this experience was a final confirmation of Jesus' victory, the affirmation of the incarnation. That which had come physically into the world had now departed, taking humanness into heaven and divinizing it. The incarnate Son of God was returning to the Godhead from which he came. It was the final and complete vindication of everything that he had lived, taught, and died for. From now on his presence would not be localized in one place or time; the saving, caring person of the Godhead became *infinitely available*. For those struggling through pain or difficulty, this possibility has a powerful psychological impact. Saving, loving power is available to us if we will allow this resurrected love to help us.

Paul said it well: "What can separate us from the love of Christ? . . . For I am convinced that nothing in death or life, in the cosmic realm of spirits, or spiritual powers both good and evil, or in the natural human world as it is or as it shall become, in the rising and setting of the stars, or in anything else in all creation, can separate us from the love of God in Christ Jesus our Lord" (Rom. 8:35-39, auth. trans.). There is nothing left to fear.

Had some modern person stood with the disciples at their joyful parting with their risen Lord, he or she might have written words like those of Howard Chandler Robbins:

> *And have the bright immensities*
> *Received our risen Lord,*
> *Where light-years frame the Pleiades*
> *And point Orion's sword?*
> *Do flaming suns his footsteps trace*
> *Through corridors sublime*
> *The Lord of interstellar space*
> *And conqueror of time?*
>
> *The heav'n that hides him from our sight*
> *Knows neither near nor far;*
> *An altar candle sheds its light*
> *As surely as a star.*
> *And where his loving people meet*
> *to share the gift divine,*
> *There stands he with unhurrying feet;*
> *There heav'nly splendors shine.*[4]

Act 6: Christ Sends the Paraclete

Before leaving his disciples in his physical form, Jesus promised them that he would send them the Paraclete, the Comforter, the Holy Spirit. In Jesus' ascension, the disciples knew intellectually the universal availability of their Lord and Savior. Now they actually experienced the universal presence of Spirit. And this outpouring was not just for a select few, a few prophets or specially gifted people. God wished to pour out his life on all who would receive him. The prophets had spoken of this outpouring for generations. This experience gave its recipients a sense of God's very being, the Holy Spirit, dwelling in and empowering them. The Spirit of God in Christ becomes incarnate in those who will receive. We have already examined the gifts of the Spirit and seen how strained our lives can be without a sense of the Holy Spirit working around us, with us, and in us. A psychologist who would have an impact on those who have been touched by this Spirit needs to know and understand the Spirit's power and to be able to help assess its reality.

So Pentecost marks the outpouring of God's Spirit in a new way. The Acts of the Apostles is the story of what happened to ordinary human beings as they were empowered from on high. When the Christian community has been most alive and vital, its people have opened themselves to receive this gift more and more completely into their labyrinthian souls. In order truly to integrate this gift into our inner being, though, we need to see the gift in the context of the events of the preceding five acts of God's drama—and even then the drama has been in vain unless we respond to it. So those psychologists who wish to guide Christians toward wholeness need to understand and aid them in their attempts to find a mature response to their experience of God's Spirit. I know only a few professional helpers who are trained well enough both psychologically and spiritually to accomplish this task, despite the fact that more and more people are seeking this kind of help. Whether we call this "spiritual guidance" or "psychological counseling" makes little difference: both of these terms describe the process of helping others bring all of their fragmented selves to God for transformation. The greatest Christian guides and the most effective psychologists, therefore, perform many of the same services.

Act 7: Our Response

The path of response for educated Westerners is not easy. We are many-leveled beings, and it takes real understanding for us to slip through the materialism in which we have been brainwashed and to start on the process of bringing ourselves and our brothers and sisters to God. The guides or companions—whether they call themselves religious or psychological—who would try to lead others of our age toward meaning, maturity, and God need first of all to be on that path themselves. The blind cannot lead the blind.

A first essential step is to know that there are few good reasons to believe only in the materialistic box. Only then are we free to step out of that box and reasonably wager our lives on the reality of the spiritual world. A second step is to choose life and love over evil, power, and death. Abbé Huvelin, the great French director of conscience, once said that we never know what brings a tree down on the side of God, but that it is most likely the quality of love those people receive.

When we really come to see the way of love as the way of God, we will want to begin courageously to act in cooperation with this love. If we are extraverted, this may incite us to plunge into social action, because we cannot stand to see the agony of the deprived, the sick, the hungry, the abused. We try to help these people and to change the systems that have oppressed them. But we often find that, try as hard as we can, we make little impression on these conditions, and unless we are continually fed from the Spirit, we may begin to lose heart. Without the Spirit's aid, we will not learn Mother Teresa's secret: "I was not called to be successful," she has said, "only faithful." And as we try to live out the prayer of St. Francis, we will surely find that it is almost impossible for us self-centered human beings to be more interested in consoling than in being consoled, in understanding than being understood, in loving than in being loved. We need to die daily and then come again and again for resurrection and new life, or we can burn out and give up. We begin to see how difficult it is to face all of ourselves and bring all this to God. I have never known anyone who could bear all of himself or herself easily, without tension. I have encountered many social-action ministers who had come to the end of their ropes and were about to abandon not only their activities, but their faith, until they returned to the never-failing springs of life that emerge from contact with the Spirit.

If we begin to see how little we have truly allowed our love to reach out to those close to us, we will come to realize how little we and our fellow human beings are like Abba, in the story of the prodigal, giving love to both the wastrel and the stuffy elder brother. It is hard for us to give up our egocentricity, which has been forged over so many years and is in fact the principal attribute that society expects us to possess, and to go the way of Abba. How many of us, though, in our own families, working environments, social groups, or churches have ever felt as if we were treated as Abba treated the prodigal and the elder brother?

Christianity is a social religion, and it recognizes that human beings are social creatures. We need one another in worship, in sharing our hopes, in confession (where we can bear one another's burdens), and especially in our failures, disappointments, and grief. One of the tragedies of the growing "elec-

tronic church'' is that it does not offer this warm human fellowship which is often the essence of healing. Dr. James Lynch
in his book *The Broken Heart* (Basic Books, 1977) has pointed
out the importance of human fellowship and communication
for our physical health and has noted that sitting next to a warm
body once a week in church has a positive physical result.

When we listen to people without judging them, we are
offering the opportunity for confession, for others to unburden
themselves and cleanse their souls. Nonjudgmental listening
is the first fruit of the practice of love.

Social action and living love are not opposed to the inner
journey and the life of prayer; they are, rather, parts of the
same reality. Our prayer withers when we do not reach out to
others, and our attempts at love falter and fail when they are
not nourished by the living water of Spirit. On both the inner
and outer ventures we need companions to support and guide
us, people with whom to share our failures, successes, and
ecstasies. Psychologists who know the spiritual dimension of
this journey will find more people seeking them than they can
deal with, and the spiritual companions who understand psychological issues—how our sexual problems and fears of
authority, for example, can damage us—will also be overbur-
dened. Both of these activities converge at the same place.

As we find that we must be more open to the spiritual way
in order to survive and love, we will also find that we need a
spiritual companion who can guide us. A richly written body
of wisdom is also available to show us our way in the spiritual
realm, just as maps show us how to travel through the physical
world.[5] We seldom come to our spiritual potential until we take
the time to stand before God—Creator, Savior and Holy
Spirit—who waits for us, eternally prepared to work the divine
transformation within us. When we stop in silence and allow
God to perform his transforming work in us, we are like trees

lifting their leaves to the sun, light transforming itself into leaf and branch and root. Jung has said that busyness is not *of* the devil, it *is* the devil. God can made us truly godlike and effective sons and daughters, but we must first be willing to turn to him quietly and prayerfully. I have found that I need at least an hour a day during which I am silently present before the Lord, or I stray off the Christian path. This time is necessary for me psychologically as well as religiously.

What do I do in that silence? First, I abide in it with gratitude that Abba with unbelievable love welcomes one such as I. Then I try to listen to what God wishes to speak in my heart. Sometimes I hear a knocking and find the risen Jesus at the door seeking to enter and talk with me. I find my own most creative time of listening to be the middle of the night, but each person needs to find the special time when he or she is most open to the Spirit.

I find that a journal open on my lap helps me to get quiet. When I am aware that God's presence is there and communicating with me, I record what is given. If God wishes to visit me and I do not record what occurs, am I taking the experience seriously? I also record dreams. Throughout biblical and early Christian times, dreams were seen as one attempt of Abba to reach out to us even when we had not specifically chosen to turn to him. (I also find that I can listen far better to God when I have learned to listen to those around me.)

When I am quiet and listening, I can then turn and enter Scripture and let the Spirit explain it. This quiet rumination in the presence of God is not in place of intellectual study and close examination of Greek or Hebrew texts; it is, rather, in addition to this serious study, a quietly personal way of allowing the Spirit that inspired the Bible to speak to us. In defeat and hopelessness we can walk with Mary Magdalene in the garden of the tomb. Tossed by life, we can feel ourselves in the ship about to flounder, and then see Jesus rise and calm the sea and wind. The possibilities for such personal entrance into the Bible are limitless, and the resultant experiences are profoundly moving. I have, in fact, found that my own most effective sermons originated in these meditative experiences of Scripture. And in a very real sense our reenactment of Jesus' death and resurrection in Eucharist is a similar stepping into the reality of the story and being of the risen Christ. My wife and I find daily Eucharist is one of the best ways of actualizing the presence of the risen Christ.

There is still another method that I use when I feel life dragging me down. I allow myself to experience the heaviness in my heart. I feel worthless, and deep within me a dark voice speaks and tells me that all effort is useless. I may try to bring my faith to bear upon these moods and attitudes, but it does not work; only when I allow the feeling to be translated into *images* that lie behind them, and then call upon the risen Jesus to calm the confusion and ugliness laid out before me, do I feel inner peace. This is a psychological process that can lead to spiritual exercise. Time after time the Christ who has defeated death and evil has come to me, and I have known again Jesus' conquering love.

This method can be taught. I give an example from a friend and a colleague, Dr. Andrew Canale, a psychologist. He has written several books, and the following illustration comes from a forthcoming book on the use of the Christian drama in the treatment of depression. Dr. Canale is depicting here his own inner experience when he was feeling anxious, fearful, pointless, dead:

> I feel sick, worthless, afraid. Scared. What is it like? I am alone. In the woods. At night. I don't know my way. I don't know where I am. The thick leaves hide the light of the moon. The darkness descends on me as if it literally has weight. I sink to the ground leaning against a tree.
>
> An owl hoots, bloodcurdling. Curdled blood sluggishly, rot-

tenly, plops through my veins, clogging rather than giving life. The dizziness of lack of oxygen sickens me and in the dizziness I hear a crackly voice.

CRACKLY VOICE: So. You have found your way here finally. Welcome to the forest of Nothing where Nothing always happens.

In my mind, the voice is like dead leaves being crunched under foot. I try to hold that picture, to help wake myself but I cannot. The voice continues.

CRACKLY VOICE: Ho ho. You try to awaken. But listen, listen carefully. There is no awakening. You are all that is. And you are Nothing. This forest is you, this moon hidden death is you. Dull, dull, dead eternity.

ME: No! No, I will not allow it. I will not accept nothingness. Anything is better than Nothing.

CRACKLY VOICE: Stupid! friend of Alice—Anything, is it? You want anything, Anything. (It is as if the dead leaves are being torn from their stems.) *Anything!*

My mind, dull though it is, is fearful. Something has occurred in this conversation that I don't understand. Something fearful. I slowly realize that it is true. Maybe Nothing is better than Anything, for Anything could be just that, virtually anything. Friend of Alice. What does the voice mean by that? As if to answer, the ground dissolves beneath me and I tumble downward, twisting, turning, somersaulting—all of which has the effect, strangely, of taking away my dizziness, of awakening me, of making me realize that I am falling somewhere, into something—dangerous. The word reminds me of the owl, or am I hearing it? No, it is laughing voices. I have entered a cage. I am surrounded by several guards who are torturing me. Hot irons come through the bars, branding my face, my back, my legs. I try to twist, to grab the irons before they burn me but the cage is too small. I am trapped. A guard speaks.

GUARD: The fool awakens. How he was so long lost in his dream I'll never know, but he'll wish he's stayed there before this is over.

The cage is on wheels. This guard pulls it toward the gate while the others continue to poke and jab at me.

Dimly, at first, I hear the sound of a crowd. Then more clearly as the cage is pulled into a coliseum. Cheers and laughter greet the arrival of the cage and its prisoner. A voice calls out.

VOICE: We have him. Let the trial begin.

SECOND VOICE: Of what is he accused?

FIRST VOICE: Of lying. Let everyone know that he is not who he says.

THIRD VOICE (from the crowd): *Har! Look at him! He has fooled no one. Let this farce of a trial be done. He is guilty. Bring on the Monster.*

CROWD (in unison): *Guilty, guilty! Bring the monster!*

FIRST VOICE: Prisoner, you are accused of lying and have been found guilty. Your punishment is to fight the Monster—to the crowd's pleasure. Let me assure you, no one has yet survived—or died quickly. For breaking the perfection of life, you are sentenced.

The guards run from the arena. I notice now that the cage is unlocked. I hurry to get out, hoping for some escape. But another gate opens simultaneously and there before me is the Monster. The crowd is in a frenzy, calling for blood, *my* blood, my now-frozen-with-fear blood. For I am staring at the Monster, and it is horrid. It is, somehow, the embodiment of the Lie of which I stand accused, an oozing solidness that simultaneously engulfs and crushes. As it approaches me, I am awestruck, for Lie though it is, it is Truth, ugly personal Truth. The strange last sentence goes through my mind as it approaches me: "For breaking the perfection of life, you are sentenced." At that, I am awakened. No, life is not perfect beyond me. The imperfection of life is not solely my fault. As I realize this, I see the deeper Truth of the Lie and that Truth is the Ultimate Lie. Toward me it moves, certain of itself, more horrible now than anything I have ever experienced, a moving condemnation of more than me, of life, a Lie so huge as to destroy by its very being. I panic and as I do, I begin to pray.

ME: O Jesus, Jesus. O Jesus, be Jesus. Be whatever Jesus is. Be here, Jesus. O sweet Jesus. However you come, then come, Jesus. Christ Almighty. Jesus Christ. Jesus.

A man stands next to me. Dressed in Palestinian peasant robe and sandals, it could be he. He speaks.

JESUS: It is I. I exist. I am here. I will help you.

He holds his hands open to the Lie. I see the sores, the holes. The Lie Monster seems, if such can be, startled. It is as if the force of his being withstands its crushing power and the holes, how can I say it? Just let the Lie pass through as if it doesn't matter. No sound comes from the crowd, or from the Monster or from me. Gradually, the Lie recedes, seeming to dissolve and the crowd departs, grumbling but unwilling to confront this stranger.

He looks at my sores, at the grime and dirt on my naked body and weeps and then he speaks.

JESUS: My dear, dear little friend. You have fallen again into the pit. You have forgotten the power of the Negative One who desires only to destroy you. But you have called me and I, servant to beggars, always heed the call of need. I am with you. Here, come here, let me heal you of your pain.

He spits on his hand and with the spit touches each sore and healing begins to come.

ME: But why, Lord, why, dear Servant, has this happened?

JESUS: You are vulnerable, alive. This is a difficult time in your life. You know your ongoing vulnerability but you forget that you are particularly vulnerable to the Lie at this time of year and when you are stressed.

ME: I have lied.

JESUS: Yes, but also you have been true. You have admitted your lies and seen the causes. Don't forget you have been pain-

fully honest with yourself. Don't give up that honesty by iden-
tifying with the Lie. For it is truly a Monster, and it is great
far beyond your sins. But fear not, for I can stand, I have stood,
I stand against it. Now let us leave this place of pain and torture
and go forth.

He puts his arm around me and leads me to a different gate.
The two of us leave the coliseum and are soon in a city street,
where he buys bread and a jug of wine and then the two of us
sit in the shade of an olive tree and share a meal.

"This active imagination," Dr. Canale writes, "broke the
spell of these powerful negative depressive feelings." As the
reader can see, this is not a technique of avoidance or denial
but rather a direct confrontation with the real problem.[6]

Personally I have used this method to withstand the on-
slaughts of inner and outer darkness. Better than any other
practice I know, it brings us to the experiential knowledge of
the saving power of Jesus' resurrection. I have written in depth
on how this method can be used in *The Other Side of Silence*
(Paulist, 1976) and given many examples there of this practice
in my own life; these examples were written not for publication
but to allow the still saving power of the risen Christ to lift
me out of intolerable darkness. Both Dr. Canale and I have
found that sometimes this is the only method that can release
many people from the oppression of depression and despair.
This process is a specifically Christian application of the practice Jung describes as "active imagination."

God came into the world, in the person of Jesus of Nazareth.
He lived and died; he met evil and defeated it by rising again.
Now, after the ascension and Pentecost, the victorious Jesus
is more available than ever before. This is psychological truth
as well as philosophical truth: "Lord, by your cross and resurrection you have set us free. You are the Savior of the
world." Psychologists as well as ministers are given the task
of enabling others to come to this freedom.

7

__ WHAT CHRISTIANITY __ CAN OFFER PSYCHOLOGY

There are many professions that offer help to struggling, hurting, and psychologically disabled human beings. A great gulf has developed, however, between those with a basic religious orientation and those whose basic emphasis has been "scientific." I see this as a false dichotomy. Of course, there are psychological problems that fall primarily within the medical and physiological province. Psyche, mind, and body are certainly interrelated. Likewise some human misery relates primarily to the "religious" realm. However, if that misery is intense enough, it will have psychological and even physiological repercussions. Physical illness or physically caused mental distress can also trigger reactions of fear and meaninglessness.

The gulf between the religious and scientific communities in the Western world was caused to a large extent by a church on the defensive. Its world view and its authority were under attack, and it responded with rigidity and inflexible dogma. In reaction, the scientific community cut itself off from the church and all religious attitudes, and most of it gradually developed in their place a rational, mechanistic materialism with no place for meaning or values. The battle lines were drawn, and the conflict continued for centuries.

The situation has changed, however, and most religious institutions are now much more open and less authoritarian. Indeed, Dr. James Lynch suggests that the church has so much accepted the attitude of the scientific world that it has lost much of its mission and direction in caring for people. On the other hand, the growing edge of the scientific community is quite uncertain about the ultimate nature of reality or how it came to be. The time has come for rapprochement and dialog between these former opponents. The religious community needs to integrate the knowledge of depth psychology into its view of human beings so that the understanding of the depth and complexity of our psyches and how we develop by stages into mature human beings is available to ministers and lay people. The church would also do well to put into practice the discoveries of the humanistic psychologists who point out the creative and healing power of love. We can learn from these professionals what love looks like in action. The best of Christians have expressed the love humanistic psychology describes. The great spiritual guides, often as directors of conscience, have instinctively known about the depth of the human soul, but neither mature Christians nor spiritual guides have clearly written much about the nature of the psyche or the nature of love and how it manifests itself. There is no doubt that the religious institutions can learn much from the psychological one, but what can psychology learn from Christianity? Before we answer that question, let us take a quick glance at the various religious and secular helping professions.

In *Companions on the Inner Way* (Crossroad, 1983), I have discussed at length the relationships between the several help-

ing professions. Psychiatry offers help to the emotionally dis-
tressed or disabled by physicians trained in medicine as well
as psychology, although some rely primarily on "psychological" methods and treatment. Psychologists, marriage, family,
and child counselors, social workers, and pastoral counselors
offer "psychological" help without the use of drugs or medical
intervention. They often work in conjunction with psychiatrists, who provide medical assistance. Clergy and lay people
(often in religious orders) may offer pastoral care to sustain
people in sorrow or crisis. Ordained clergy offer sacramental
ministrations, Eucharist, reconciliation, and the laying on of
hands, are sometimes quite effective. Spiritual guides or spiritual directors offer two quite different kinds of companionship
on the inner journey. The following charts from *Companions
on the Inner Way* describe the different reasons for these relationships, and the various goals, methods, and personal relationships that are found in each of these encounters.

The Goals and Direction of Therapy

What is the task of the "helper," the psychological healer,
the therapist? Is it to "fix" others, alleviate their pain, enable
them to manage their outer lives, and adjust them to our sometimes crazy society? Or is it to accompany people on the way
to maturity, wholeness, and human fulfillment? John Sanford,
a professional analyst and counselor, reported that many of the
people who come to him professionally for help stop their
therapy when they are no longer suffering. Yet this may be
the very moment when real steps toward integration, wholeness, and religious meaning might be achieved. Indeed, what
is human fulfillment? In Chapter 2 we suggested that Richard
Coan's description of the optimal personality was the best that
we had encountered. He concluded that truly whole people are
characterized by efficiency (are disciplined and effective), are

	Psychiatry	**Pastoral Counseling Psychotherapy Social Case Work**	**Pastoral Care**
Reason for Encounter	Person in pain, with inner conflicts, psychosomatic disease, or unable to fit in social group.	Person with same symptoms, but needing neither drugs nor a controlled environment. Can work with psychiatrist.	Reaching out to people in psychic pain, loneliness, grief. Initial contact may come from pastor.
Goal	To remove pain and enable person to function adequately within himself or herself and within the more intimate and larger social group. Except in case of disoriented persons, the patient decides termination of relationship.	Same goal as psychiatry, but limited to those who do not need drugs and custodial care. To provide insight and self-determination.	To bring comfort, renewal, relief of pain and sorrow and confusion, but without necessarily bringing insight.
Method	Any method necessary to bring healing, even understanding of world view and spiritual discipline, but usually relying on custodial care and psychotherapy. Should be aware of existential roots of some problems and have a place for religion to avoid a limited point of view. Often uses chemical intervention. Sometimes utilizes dream analysis.	With the exception of use of drugs and custodial care, uses the same methods as psychiatrist. One works within a religious framework; the other has no necessary religious connection, but should be aware of religious and existential dimension of psychosomatic and psychic distress. Stops process at limits set by patient.	Concerned caring in one-to-one calling or in arranged social gatherings and fellowship, in study or prayer or sociality. Within Christian tradition usually connected with priesthood, but not necessarily with pastoral counseling or spiritual direction A or B. Takes seeker no further than he or she asks.
Personal Relationship to Seeker	Healing seldom occurs unless there is genuine care and humility. Not necessary for use of medical model, but still helpful.	The therapist's only scalpel is his or her personality. Caring, humility, and knowledge are all necessary.	Concerned caring with enough awareness not to encourage dependency.

	Priesthood	Spiritual Direction A: Apophatic-Nonmediational	Spiritual Direction B: Kataphatic-Mediational Shamanistic
Reason for Encounter	Providing sacrament, assistance in experiencing God, or healing of body or mind. In most cases initiated by seeker.	A soul searching for God without any obvious disorder or acute need. Always initiated by seeker.	A psyche in pain seeking for integration of body, mind, and soul and release from pain. Usually initiated by seeker.
Goal	To achieve whatever goal is desired by individual.	Being and becoming in God without essential consideration of personal psychological problems. Particularly useful for once-born type as described by James. Never goes beyond individual's goals.	To alleviate the pain so person can function, to bring insight into how pain is related to inner journey, and to facilitate that journey. To continue with person as long as needed to bring individual to sustaining fellowship with God. Can offer goals.
Method	Providing individual and group sacraments, arranging worship, mediating of the Holy. Within Christian tradition this role is traditionally connected with pastoral care and even with spiritual directions A and B. Providing confession, absolution, Eucharist, anointing, etc.	Allowing self and relationship to be a vehicle of grace, of the will of God. Primary method: surrender, letting go whatever is in God's way. Abiding with the person making the journey. Referral of any significant problem to psychiatrist or therapist-counselor.	Whatever is needed to facilitate the individual through pains on the way. Usually will not deal with psychotics and will be equipped with knowledge of pastoral care and pastoral counseling. Will be particularly equipped to deal with existential problems. Will use psychiatrists as consultants and will be so used by enlightened psychiatrists or therapists. Can use sacramental actions.
Personal Relationship to Seeker	Need be none, but in Christian framework it is a necessary ingredient if priest is a mediator of Christ.	Only God is responsible for whatever healing/growth occurs. "*Thy will be done.*"	God gives transformation, but shaman/guide is mediator of experience, knowledge, critical understanding, and divine love.

creative, possess inner harmony, relate well and in depth to other human beings, and are in touch with that reality which transcends the ordinary world.

At least four of these qualities have specifically religious overtones. In creativity something new emerges in the individual, and that person shares in the nature of the creating divine. One of the most frequent goals of Eastern religion is the achieving of some inner harmony. We have seen how central relatedness is when God's nature is ultimately perceived as love. Most religions are trying to open us human beings to transcendence. Even in regard to efficiency or effectiveness— few people possess this quality more than those seized with a religious mission. At this point it is wise to remember Coan's statement that secular psychology, when it is consistent, cannot offer goals and establish values about the optimal life.

On the other hand, we have already noted the fact that few psychological professionals are comfortable with religious issues and data, and few initiate questions about it. If religion is a natural part of life, it should no more be avoided than questions dealing with sexuality and hostility. We have already described in some detail the importance that Jung and most of his followers attribute to a vital religious connection in healthy humans. Dr. Robert McCully, a professor of psychiatry at the Medical University of South Carolina, takes his profession to task for ignoring the important religious dimension of life and draws heavily upon Jung and the sociologist Emile Durkheim.[1] Roger Walsh has both a medical degree and a Ph.D. in psychology and is a professor in Psychiatry at the Medical School at Irvine, California. He has written several books on the importance of the religious factors in human wholeness. His views have been summarized in the *American Journal of Psychiatry* (137 [1980]: 663-673). He maintains that we must take the transpersonal experiences seriously if we are to deal with the whole person and aid that whole person to come to fruition.[2]

Dr. Harry M. Tiebout has written extensively on the importance of religious commitment and experience in overcoming alcoholism, one of the most serious and disabling diseases on the American scene.[3]

What specifically does the Christian religion have to offer to the health and wholeness of human beings and to those who would bring human beings to wholeness? The Christianity I am referring to I have described as the Christian cosmic drama. I am all too well aware that few people have really lived the full implications of this kind of Christianity. The statement is trite, but true, that Christianity has not so much failed as it has seldom been seriously tried. We see Christians who are that in name only and who have never seriously decided to follow the Christian directive of love; some of these are found in high places within religious institutions. And there are those who feel that since salvation is so freely available, they don't have to do anything to receive it. On the other hand, there are those so convinced that the Holy Spirit is moving within them that they don't have to make any conscious decisions or actions; they abrogate all personal responsibility. The failure of the church to reach out to the poor, the imprisoned, the broken, the mentally disturbed, all those who are different from the average, is a scandal. We have done little to change the social systems which create this havoc. As a Christian church and society we have not lived out Jesus' message.

What can we do as Christians and as a church? We can face our brokenness and failures as Christians, bear the tension of our imperfect faith and action and of our imperfect institutions, and try to live more fully within the divine drama. We need to work at our Christian vocation as if our entire salvation depended upon it. At the same time we have the paradoxical faith that we are loved and saved purely by grace. When the cosmic drama of Christ is truly understood, we are placed in this creative tension, and miracles occur in us and in those around us.

This kind of living has produced saints throughout the ages, and most saints were healing people. What are the characteristics of this kind of healing life? What are the psychological implications of Christianity?

The Psychological Implications of Christianity

Writing about the implications of Christianity for psychology is an awesome task, because it suggests that the writer knows something about the essential nature of both of these disciplines. It requires particular temerity on my part, as I am neither a shining example of psychological maturity, on the one side, or of Christian perfection, on the other. However, I undertake the task because I was asked to do so and because I have been much involved in both areas, and I am continually striving to grow to greater wholeness in both.

First of all, Christianity presents a view of the universe, a world view, a view of the ultimate nature of things that has touched the lives of many people and gives meaning to all human beings in the world and to the world itself. Although most modern psychologists reject that world view, they have certainly not come up with any satisfactory alternatives. Neither rational materialism nor humanism gives any ultimate meaning to life. If I were to adopt a world view other than that of Christianity, it would be neither of these, but rather that of Eastern religion.

We have outlined our view of the essential nature of Christianity in the last two chapters. The Christian cosmic drama tells of a creator God who is the ultimate source of all reality, both physical and spiritual. This God is characterized by the love expressed by the father in Jesus' story of the prodigal son and the elder brother. It was expressed by Jesus' outreach to the poor and dispossessed, his compassion toward and healing of the sick and demon-possessed, his courage and honesty, his sacrificial death and resurrection, and his sending of the Holy Spirit. God created with love that love might be born, and so the Divine Lover of necessity gave freedom; real love is possible only in the context of freedom. One part of God's created universe rebelled like an adolescent and dragged others away from love and God. The result was evil in the world that God had created good, and so God reentered the world to defeat evil and free us from its power. Then the resurrected Lord poured out his Spirit in a new way upon humankind.

Our human Christian task is to know the reality of that love, to respond to that love, to receive it, and then share it with other people—each in our own unique way. Each of us has an eternal destiny with a life that extends beyond this physical time-bound world. We are amazing creatures, amphibious creatures, who bridge the physical and spiritual worlds and have the ability to perceive in ways beyond the five physical senses. We are also growing creatures who go through many stages of development before we come to our ultimate maturity and destiny.

If this is an accurate picture of reality (and it is the most complete picture of which I am aware), then the task of the psychologist is to help the individual (or group) be free from those things that inhibit growth and development—mental illness, drug abuse, immaturity, neuroses, compulsions, and unrealistic fears—and help them adjust to the full measure of reality and possible creative experience that surrounds us. If human beings have an eternal destiny, part of the task of human helpers is to facilitate their journey toward that destiny. Dr. Riklin wrote that just because a person was dying was no reason to stop analysis.

What would we look for in a psychologist who was operating from this basic view of reality? What abilities, qualities of personality, what knowledge, what kind of vision and understanding would we expect to find?

First of all, we would expect that person to be fully equipped with a good background of how human beings grow and develop psychosexually and in relationships; how they can function efficiently and adequately; how they can be freed from crippling problems created by poverty, neglect, or childhood trauma; how they can come to intimacy; how they can learn to listen and communicate; how they can come to genuine satisfaction with life; how they can get along in the world; and how they can find a meaningful goal for themselves. They will recognize that human beings are very different and have different ways to follow. *In addition the psychologist who is dealing with the whole person will know that there is a transcendental realm and a Divine Lover to be found there and how this saving, guiding reality and Spirit can be encountered.* Many people are turning to psychologists for this last kind of knowledge because they have found more understanding and help and love in psychologists' offices than they have found in the churches, and they want to enter upon the spiritual journey in the same kind of framework.

To ask psychologists to know this other dimension and how to deal with it may sound like an impossible request. When I was with Jung and asked him why he got involved in religious matters, he replied that people came to him suffering from sicknesses caused by a loss of meaning. He sent them back to their pastors, who did not know how to help them. When they returned still suffering, he concluded that if he were to facilitate healing, he had to deal with matters of religion. Psychologists need to know all they can about the purely physical and psychological causes of illness. They also need to know the range and depth of human experience and to use the same critical and open attitude toward these nonphysical experiences that they use toward sense data. The only way that they can do this is by trying to follow some religious tradition fully and listening to and trying to understand their own paranormal and religious experiences. At the same time, theologians and pastors need to be widely acquainted with the findings of clinical psychology and be available when psychologists find areas in which they are not competent.

Not only can the blind not lead the blind, but none of us can lead a person farther on the path toward maturity or spiritual fulfillment than we have gone ourselves. Yet since no one who understands the nature of the ideal Christian life would claim to be very far upon that path, we will reach out in humility to those who come to us. We are part of a broken world and carry within us a large measure of the world's corruption. We are in no position to judge or condemn any other human being. We look down on no one. We believe that the compassionate love expressed by Christ is our best instrument for enabling the Spirit dwelling in each person to blaze into a living flame.

As facilitators of wholeness, we will try to live on the growing edge of life led by the Spirit. We shall try to bring our lives into harmony with the love expressed in Christ. This requires discipline; we will try to restrain our sensuality, our self-seeking and arrogance, our hostility, which is so often a reaction to fear. We will try to be angry and sin not. We will at the same time try to extend to ourselves the same compassion and love that we extend to others. We will fail in both of these endeavors many times and pick ourselves up and try again. Paul Clasper says it well: "We need to be firm with ourselves, knowing how easily we can be diverted from our quest; but we need, equally, to be gentle with ourselves. We know that we cannot roughly coerce others; this only provokes resistance. Why do we treat ourselves in ways we know we cannot treat others? We would do better to do unto ourselves as we would, at our best, do unto others. We give them place and time. We should treat ourselves with the same courtesy."[4] Jung has said that a psychiatrist is a surgeon whose only scalpel is his or her own personality. If we continue to hate ourselves, we are likely to project upon others what we cannot stand in ourselves.

If we are operating from a Christian model, we will want to know our model well. We will try to know the teachings and life of Jesus and the religious background of which he was a part. Carl Schurz has said: "Ideals are like stars; you will not succeed in touching them with your hands, but like the seafaring person on the desert of waters, you choose them as your guides, and, following them, you reach your destiny." We must know the nature of our star if we are to follow it.

The redwood tree grows from the tiniest seed and becomes one of the largest living things by exposing itself to the light of the sun. Daily it spreads out its branches and takes in the light and turns it into a living, material tree. We need to expose ourselves to the presence of the loving God daily and receive the love that can lift us up out of darkness and can build our lives with the same enduring reality as the redwood. Whenever those of us who are trying to operate from this model are with another, we will try to be aware that this loving Spirit is present within and between both of us. We will also realize that the transformations that sometimes take place are often as much in spite of us as because of us, and that the Spirit has to use imperfect instruments, because God has no other instruments to use.

Christianity offers not only a hopeful map of reality, but also gives us a way to move towards the treasure the map reveals: love. Love is a great mystery.[5] Few are the people who can love humanity until they have allowed themselves to be captured by the love of one other human being. Paul has written an excellent anatomy of love in 1 Corinthians 13. In his first letter John tells us that we cannot love God if we do not love our brothers and sisters.

Modern psychology has added to our understanding of love.

Love is not just what we feel, but what we do. Also we cannot love another to whom we do not listen. Our first sign of acceptance is our willingness to listen. Then we can begin to communicate ourselves, our brokenness, our hopes, our caring, our experiences of the Divine Lover. Communication is impossible without honesty and truthful encounter, but honesty must always be subject to love and given only at the right time and in love. In its emphasis on the importance of love, psychology has drawn more deeply on Christian thought than it sometimes acknowledges.

None of us can go this way alone. We would not even be human except for our experience of being nurtured as children in some family and culture. We cannot go far on the spiritual journey alone. If we are to grow, we need one another. Only as I have someone with whom I do share *all* of myself, am I a fit and safe person for others to share with. Then I also need a wider fellowship of which I can feel a part. I need to be part of a religious community. All this roots me firmly in the human family and the human condition.

Human beings cannot live by bread alone. If we are to be fully alive, we need our symbols and our rituals. Few people come to their potential destiny who do not have living symbols that enliven them and guide them. I have found that the most living symbol and ritual for me is that of Eucharist, in which I listen to the wisdom of the tradition and then participate in the reenactment of Christ rising out of death into resurrection and sharing that life with me. For some people the Christian symbols have been defaced by Christians they have known (usually in childhood), and they need to find others to replace those that have been destroyed. If one is not alienated from the Christian symbols, they are worth considering.

Paul wrote that love never ceases, never fails, never comes to an end. How can the psychologist who thinks that life ends with the grave truly comfort the person who is dying, cut off in the midst of life? Or indeed anyone who faces death? If our lives do continue—and there is good evidence for that possibility—then the psychologists who do not prepare us for continual growth in this crisis through which we all pass are not dealing honestly with their patients. They simply cannot give the final encouragement that often enables us to bear the tension and pain of our imperfections, our ugliness, and the tragedies that occur in nearly every life.[6] If we believe that the loving and redeeming risen Christ is working in and through us and the world, then we can never know until the end of time what have been the effects of our actions and our intentions. Everything may be redeemed, and all may be well at last.

The prospect of an eternal destiny has a fearful aspect as well as being a source of hope. We come to know the murky depth of ourselves as we pause and reflect. I wonder if we can reflect as deeply as we need to unless we keep some kind of written reflection, some kind of journal. There we can record our reflections on how we have treated those around us. We can listen to our dreams that tell us of the often-forgotten depths of ourselves. We can reflect upon the complaints and words of appreciation of those whose lives are intermeshed with ours. Then we can also consider how little we do in a world full of poverty, hatred, strife, and warfare. We are a part of this world, and all suffering human beings are our neighbors. What courage it takes for us to face this! However, as we do, and still seek to follow our star, we can be companions with others who seek to be free of their impediments toward growth and to work toward full human lives, toward an eternal destiny.

The task set before anyone who would deal with the whole human being—body, mind, and soul—is a gigantic one. But the incredible beauty and value of the human being is worth all that we can give—and much more.

NOTES

Chapter 1: No Room for God in Psychology and Healing

1. *San Francisco Chronicle,* October 3, 1984.
2. *Clinical Psychiatry News* (March 1981), p. 28, as quoted in Gerald May, *Care of Mind/Care of Spirit* (New York: Harper & Row, 1982), p. 167.
3. The July 1982 issue of *Science Digest* contains an article by John Gliedman, "Scientists in Search of the Soul," that reviews the thinking of several leading theorists in science.
4. As quoted in May, pp. 142-143.
5. There is an interesting attempt to trace the unconscious of Freud to physiological roots. Kevin McKean has surveyed several recent books showing the physical basis of the unconscious mind in the article, "In Search of Unconscious Mind," *Discover* (February 1985).
6. C. William Tageson, *Humanistic Psychology: A Synthesis* (Homewood, Ill.: Dorsey, 1982), p. ix.
7. This and the following quotations are from Paul Vitz, *Psychology as Religion: The Cult of Self-Worship* (Grand Rapids: Eerdmans, 1977), pp. 18-27, 76-77.

Chapter 2: A Place for God in Psychology

1. William James, *The Varieties of Religious Experience* (New York: Longman, Green and Co., 1920), p. 204.
2. C. G. Jung, *Collected Works,* vol. 11 (Princeton, N.J.: Princeton, 1978), p. 334.

3. *Jung Letters,* vol. 1 (Princeton, N.J.: Princeton, 1973), p. 377.

4. *Jung Letters,* vol. 2, p. 435.

5. C. G. Jung, *Two Essays in Analytical Psychology* (New York: Meridian Books, 1956), pp. 215-216.

6. Quoted by Vera van der Heydt, *Jung and Religion* (London: Guild of Pastoral Psychology, n.d.), pp. 9ff.

7. Hans Schaer's book *Religion and the Cure of Souls in Jung's Psychology* (New York: Pantheon, 1950), has shown Jung's deep admiration and respect for the dogma and practice of Christianity, particularly pp. 161-167.

8. C. G. Jung, *Memories, Dreams, Reflections* (New York: Pantheon, 1963), pp. 210-211.

9. Van der Heydt, pp. 13ff.

10. Jung was asked by a study group in Los Angeles why he never dealt with the subject of Jesus' resurrection. His answer is to be found in vol. 18 of *The Collected Works,* entitled "The Symbolic Life," pp. 692-696, written February 19, 1954. His treatment of the subject is weak and rationalistic. He did not see how the event could have been a historical event, so he treated it as only a psychological event. He did not even consider that it could have been a synchronistic event, *both* psychological *and* physical. That Jung did not apply this principle to the resurrection suggests to me that he had an emotional block on the subject.

11. Jung, *Memories, Dreams, Reflections,* p. 354.

12. On September 22, 1944, he wrote to H. Irminger of Zürich, explaining why he was not a Catholic, but he did not send the letter, and it was found among his papers. It is printed in vol. 18 of *The Collected Works,* pp. 645-647. Jung maintained that he was "a practical Christian to whom love and justice to his brother mean more than dogmatic speculation about whose ultimate truth or untruth no human being can ever have certain knowledge. The relation to my brother and the unity of the true 'catholic' Christendom is to me infinitely more important than 'justification by *fide sola*.' " Jung was still reacting to his father. Murray Stein has provided an excellent study of Jung and his relationship to Christianity in his recent book, *Jung's Treatment of Christianity* (Evanston, Ill.: Chiron Publications, 1985).

13. Roy W. Fairchild, "Psychology, Humanity, and Ministry," *Phos* (Christmas 1984), p. 3. *Phos* is published by Trinity Institute, 74 Trinity Place, New York NY 10006.

Chapter 3: Living in an Open Universe

1. John Keller, *Let Go, Let God* (Minneapolis: Augsburg, 1985), p. 32.
2. Andrew M. Greeley, *The Sociology of the Paranormal: A Reconnaissance*, Sage Research Papers in the Social Studies, Studies in Religion and Ethnicity Series, vol. 3, series no. 90-023 (Beverly Hills and London: Sage Publications).
3. I am deeply grateful to Finney, who was present at the Finch lecture, for sharing his dissertation research on this subject. The most important of these are: the many studies of R. W. Hood, Jr., *Journal for the Scientific Study of Religion* 9:285-291; 13:65-71; 14:29-41; 17:279-287; *Psychological Reports* (1973) 33:549-550; 39:1127-2236; 44:804-806; *Review of Religious Research* 17:179-188; 18:264-270; N. G. Holm, *Journal for the Scientific Study of Religion* 21:268-276; G. Lea, *Journal of Religion and Health* (1982) 336-351; Orlo Strunk Jr., *Mature Religion: A Psychological Study* (New York: Abingdon, 1965).
4. Vol. 12, no. 2 (1973):209-221.
5. The work of Robert G. Jahn, Princeton's dean of Engineering, and his assistants in the Engineering Anomalies Research Laboratory in the School of Engineering/Applied Science at Princeton is the most extensive work in this field that I know of. Both in gathering data and in providing theory, this group has provided a comprehensive exposition of the subject. Their monographs are available on request. And *The Mind Race* by Russell Targ and Keith Harary (New York: Villard Books, 1984) is the most up-to-date report of the work of the Institute for Noetic Sciences in Palo Alto; this work began at Stanford Research Institute and has continued.
6. Werner Heisenberg, *Physics and Philosophy: The Revolution in Modern Science* (New York: Harper & Row, 1958), pp. 200ff.
7. Paul Davies, *God and the New Physics* (New York: Simon and Schuster, 1984).

8. *British Journal of Medical Psychology,* as quoted by Flanders Dunbar, *Emotions and Bodily Changes,* 4th ed. (New York: Columbia Univ., 1954), pp. 83-84.

9. Jerome D. Frank, *Persuasion and Healing* (New York: Schocken, 1963), pp. 233-234. See the evidence he gives on p. 61.

Chapter 4: Many Worlds of Experience and Ways of Knowing Them

1. Aldous Huxley, *Doors of Perception* (New York: Harper & Row, 1970), pp. 22-24. Reprinted by permission of Harper & Row, Publishers, Inc., Mrs. Laura Huxley, and Chatto & Windus.

2. Paul G. Hiebert, *Missiology: An International Review,* vol. 10, no. 1 (January 1982):35-47.

3. Dr. J. Andrew Canale's two published books are *Masters of the Heart* (New York: Paulist, 1978) and *The Human Jesus* (New York: Paulist, 1985).

4. A complete list of these passages in each of the books of the New Testament is found in the appendix of my book *Encounter with God.* My books dealing with the gifts are, first of all, *Encounter with God,* a theology of gifts. *God, Dreams and Revelation; Dreams, a Way to Listen to God; The Other Side of Silence: A Guide to Christian Meditation;* and *Afterlife—The Other Side of Dying* deal with revelation. *Healing and Christianity* deals with healing and miracles. *Discernment, a Study in Ecstasy and Evil* and *The Christian and the Supernatural* study the gifts of discernment and of wisdom and knowledge. *Tongue Speaking* deals with prophecy and tongues. *Caring: How Can We Love One Another?* is an examination of the most important of all the Christian gifts.

Chapter 5: Christianity As Healing Love and Hope

1. I have described this cosmic drama in much greater depth in my recent book *Resurrection: Release from Oppression* (Ramsey, N.J.: Paulist, 1985).

2. Harold Goddard, *The Meaning of Shakespeare,* vol. 2 (Chicago: Univ. of Chicago, 1965), p. 208.

3. C. G. Jung, *Modern Man in Search of a Soul* (New York: Harcourt Brace Jovanovich, 1955), pp. 234-235.

4. Raymond E. Brown, *The Birth of the Messiah* (Garden City, N.Y.: Doubleday, 1977), esp. pp. 25-38.

5. Walter Wink, "And the Lord Appeared First to Mary: Sexual Politics in the Resurrection Witness," in *Social Themes of the Christian Year: A Commentary on the Lectionary,* ed. Dieter T. Hessel (Philadelphia: Geneva Press, 1983), pp. 177-182.

6. C. G. Jung, *The Symbolic Life,* vol. 18 in *Collected Works* (Princeton, N.J.: Princeton, 1976), pp. 265-290.

7. *Pacific Theological Review,* vol. 16, no. 3 (Spring 1983): 19-26.

8. I know of few more powerful and dramatic portrayals of the life, death, and resurrection of Jesus than Dr. Canale's book *The Human Jesus* (Ramsey, N.J.: Paulist, 1985). The very wholeness of the human being, Jesus of Nazareth, points beyond the human to the divine.

Chapter 6: Christianity as Redeeming and Transforming Love

1. Pinchas Lapide, *The Resurrection of Jesus: A Jewish Perspective* (Minneapolis: Augsburg, 1983).

2. In my recent book *Resurrection: Release from Oppression* (Ramsey, N.J.: Paulist, 1985) I deal in depth with the implications of this event for fragile human beings.

3. David Stanley, "Contemplation of the Gospels, Ignatius Loyola, and the Contemporary Christian," *Theological Studies* 29 (1969): 417-443. This kind of active imagination Bible study is clearly summarized by Gerald O'Collins in his book *What Can We Say about Resurrection?* (Ramsey, N.J.: Paulist, 1978).

4. *The Hymnal of the Episcopal Church in the U.S.A.* (Greenwich, Conn.: Seabury, 1943), no. 354. Words reprinted by permission of Morehouse Barlow Co., Inc.

5. In many of my books I have mentioned the spiritual reading that has been most helpful to me, but particularly in the text and bibliography of *Encounter with God; The Other Side of Silence; Prophetic Ministry; Adventure Inward;* and *Companions on the Inner Way.*

6. In the chapter entitled "Windows Inward" in *The Other Side of Silence* I have given several examples of this kind of image praying, as well as in *Companions on the Inner Way* and *Adventure Inward*.

Chapter 7: What Christianity Can Offer Psychology

1. *Directions in Psychiatry*, vol. 4 (New York: Hatherleigh Company, Ltd., n.d.).
2. Roger Walsh, "The Consciousness Disciplines and the Behavioral Sciences: Questions of Comparison and Assessment," *American Journal of Psychiatry* 137 (1980): 663-673.
3. Harry M. Tiebout, *Ego Factors in Surrender,* is available along with other papers by Dr. Tiebout from Hazelden Educational Services, Box 176, Center City MN 55012.
4. Paul and Janet Clasper, *The Ox Herder Pictures* (Hong Kong: Lotus-Logos Press, 6-8, Garden Road, n.d.), p. 13.
5. In my book *Caring: How Can We Love One Another?* (New York: Paulist, 1981), I deal with the subject of love in depth.
6. In *The Christian and the Supernatural* (Minneapolis: Augsburg, 1976), and in *Afterlife: The Other Side of Dying* (New York: Crossroad, 1982), I deal with the subject of having knowledge of another dimension of reality. In the latter book I give a picture of the Christian view of afterlife.

FOR FURTHER READING

A. Religion and Psychology

1. In the December 1984 issue of *Phos*, Trinity Institute, New York, Dr. Fairchild sketched the development of an overenthusiastic acceptance of psychology by the Christian establishment to a serious questioning of the influence of some psychologies on religion.

Two early books were enthusiastic about the relationship:

Outler, Albert. *Psychotherapy and the Christian Message.* New York: Harper, 1954. (Out of print.)

Roberts, David. *Psychotherapy and a Christian View of Man.* New York: Scribners, 1950. (Out of print.)

Three books raised questions about the relationship:

Menninger, Karl. *Whatever Became of Sin?* New York: Dutton, 1973.

Pruyser, Paul. *The Minister as Diagnostician: Personal Problems in Pastoral Perspective.* Philadelphia: Westminster, 1976.

Reiff, Phillip. *The Triumph of the Therapeutic.* New York: Harper and Row, 1968. (Out of print.)

A spate of books in recent years have been critical of the point of view of psychology.

Cosgrove, Mark. *Psychology Gone Awry: An Analysis of Psychological World Views.* Grand Rapids: Zondervan, 1978. (Out of print.)

131

Gross, Martin. *The Psychological Society: A Critical Analysis of Psychiatry, Psychotherapy, Psychoanalysis and the Psychological Revolution.* New York: Random House, 1979. (Out of print.)

Kilpatrick, William. *Psychological Seduction: The Failure of Modern Psychology.* New York: Nelson, 1983.

Myers, David. *The Inflated Self: Human Illusions and the Biblical Call to Hope.* New York: Winston/Seabury, 1980.

Vitz, Paul. *Psychology as Religion: The Cult of Self-Worship,* Grand Rapids: Eerdmans, 1977.

Zilbergeld, Bernie. *The Shrinking of America: Myths of Psychological Change,* Boston: Little Brown, 1983.

2. Richard Coan has presented an excellent survey of modern psychological theory with special reference to the optimal personality and that naturally involves the religious orientation of that point of view.

Coan, Richard. *Hero, Artist, Sage or Saint?: A Survey of Views on What Is Variously Called Mental Health, Normality, Maturity, Self-Actualization, and Human Fulfillment.* New York: Columbia, 1977.

Three classic studies of the relationship of Christianity and psychology are:

Freud, Sigmund. *The Future of an Illusion.* New York: Norton, 1975.

James, William. *The Varieties of Religious Experience.* New York: Macmillan, 1961.

Jung, Carl. *Psychology and Religion, West and East,* 2nd ed., vol. 2 in *Collected Works.* Princeton, N.J.: Princeton, 1969. (This will be more understandable if one reads the books listed in the next section prior to reading this volume.)

3. I have tried to present the relationship between Jungian thought and Christianity in *Christo-Psychology* (New York: Crossroad,

1982); *Prophetic Ministry* (New York: Crossroad, 1982); and *Companions on the Inner Way* (New York: Crossroad, 1984).

Gerald May presents quite a different point of view in *Care of Mind, Care of Spirit: Psychiatric Dimensions of Spiritual Direction* (San Francisco: Harper and Row, 1982).

4. James Lynch connects medicine, psychology, and religion in:

Lynch, James. *The Broken Heart*. New York: Basic Books, 1977.

B. Psychological Thought

1. Coan's book mentioned above gives an excellent survey of the main lines of psychological thought.

2. The various schools of psychological thought in more depth. For an up-to-date presentation of the biomedical view of human beings see:

Konner, Melvin. *The Tangled Wing: Biological Constraints on the Human Spirit*. New York: Holt, Rinehart and Winston, 1982.

Behaviorism is presented by B. F. Skinner in a best-selling novel and in his theory of value:

Walden Two. New York: Macmillan, 1948. (Out of print.) *Beyond Freedom and Dignity*. New York: Bantam, 1972.

An excellent summary of the many hues of humanistic psychology is presented in:

Tageson, C. William. *Humanistic Psychology: A Synthesis*. Homewood, Ill.: Dorsey, 1982.

Freud presented his basic theory in two books:
The Interpretation of Dreams. New York: Avon, 1967.
Introductory Lectures on Psychoanalysis. New York: Liveright, 1977.

A violent controversy has raged over the Freud Archives and has been thoroughly discussed in *The New Yorker*, December 5 and December 12, 1983, under "Trouble in the Archives."

The thought of Jung is complex, and Jung's books need to be read in the following order if Jung is to be understood:

Memories, Dreams, Reflections. New York: Random, 1965.

Man and His Symbols. New York: Dell, 1968.

The Tavistock Lectures on the Theory and Practice of Analytical Psychology. vol. 18 in *Collected Works.* Princeton, N.J.: Princeton, 1976.

Modern Man in Search of a Soul. New York: Harcourt Brace Jovanovich, 1955.

Two Essays on Analytical Psychology. vol. 7 in *Collected Works.* Princeton, N.J.: Princeton, 1972.

One can then go on to *Psychology and Religion: West and East, Civilization in Transition,* and his other writings.

3. Four excellent studies of Jung's thought and its religious implications are:

Clift, Wallace. *Jung and Christianity: The Challenge of Reconciliation.* New York: Crossroad, 1982.

Schaer, Hans. *Psychotherapy and the Cure of Souls in the Psychology of Jung.* New York: Pantheon, 1950. (Out of print.)

Welch, John L. *Spiritual Pilgrims: Carl Jung and Teresa of Avila.* New York: Paulist, 1982.

Stein, Murray. *Jung's Treatment of Christianity.* Evanston, Ill.: Chiron Publications, 1985.

C. Toward a New World View

1. Modern physics has broken down many of our ordinary ideas about the world in which we live. By mapping the process of scientific change, Kuhn shows how new facts are revealed and thus comes to a new view of the world. Heisenberg, one of the greatest physicists of all time, detailed how the changes came about in physics and how this understanding can open up a new view of reality. Davies

has brought us in touch with the latest thinking in physics. Toben has provided cartoons to make these new insights comprehensible.

Davies, Paul. *God and the New Physics.* New York: Simon and Schuster, 1983.

Heisenberg, Werner. *Physics and Philosophy: The Revolution in Modern Science.* World Perspectives Series. New York: Harper & Row, 1958.

Kuhn, Thomas S. *The Structure of Scientific Revolutions,* 2nd ed. Chicago: Univ. of Chicago, 1970.

Toben, Bob and Wolf, Fred A. *Space-Time and Beyond.* New York: Bantam.

2. Two indispensable works that delineate the uses and limitations of language and logic in our search for knowledge are:

Ayer, Alfred Jules. *Language, Truth and Logic.* 2nd ed. New York: Dover, 1936.

Johnson, Kenneth G. *General Semantics: An Outline Survey.* San Francisco: International Society for General Semantics, 1972.

3. In *Encounter with God, Healing and Christianity, Prophetic Ministry, Christo-Psychology, Companions on the Inner Way,* and *Afterlife* I have sketched out this world view, as the data that I present is not meaningful except in terms of a new world view. In *Encounter with God* I also show by a survey of the history of thought how we fell into the materialistic world view. I also provide a theory of perception based in part on the following four excellent studies:

Huxley, Aldous. *Doors of Perception.* New York: Harper & Row, 1970.

Lovejoy, Arthur O. *The Revolt Against Dualism.* 2nd ed. New York: Open Court, 1960. This brilliant study of human knowing opens the door to a broader view of how knowledge is acquired than is usually recognized in our culture.

Whyte, Lancelot. *The Unconscious before Freud.* Classics in Psychology and Psychiatry Series. Dover, N.H.: Frances Pinter, 1978. A survey of the twisting path towards recognition of a

realm of largely unconscious experience and the questions that
have thus been opened up.

Weil, Andrew. *The Natural Mind: A New Way of Looking at Drugs
and the Higher Consciousness*. Boston: Houghton Mifflin,
1972. Weil suggested that we will not begin to solve the growing
drug problem until we are ready to deal with the need for altered
states of consciousness.

D. Gifts of the Spirit and Religious Experience

1. Almost all major religious groups have maintained that divine
influences are manifested in the ordinary physical world. Dodds
showed that the Greeks (usually considered the paragons of ration-
ality) were as irrational as the Hebrews and other people. I have
presented a theoretical base in "Miracles in the Western World" in
The Encyclopedia of Religion, ed. by Miracea Eliade, New York:
Macmillan Publishing Co., to be published in late 1985.

Dodds, E. R. *The Greeks and the Irrational*. Sather Classical
Lectures, no. 25. Berkeley: University of California, 1951.

Kelsey, Morton. *Resurrection: Release from Oppression*. Ramsey,
N.J.: Paulist, 1985. Presents a more fully developed world view
in which the resurrection of Jesus and the gifts of the Spirit are
meaningful.

2. For the last 20 years I have presented studies of the various
gifts of the Spirit simply because no careful studies had been done
within a framework that made sense in our modern world. I have
also referred to these in the text.

Healing

Kelsey, Morton. *Healing and Christianity*. New York: Harper &
Row, 1973. This was the result of 20 years of study and research.

Revelation

Kelsey, Morton. *God, Dreams and Revelation*. Minneapolis:
Augsburg, 1974. The original edition *Dreams, The Dark Speech*

of the Spirit (1968) contains an appendix of early Christian statements about dreams and revelation in general.

Kelsey, Morton. *Dreams: A Way to Listen to God.* Ramsey, N.J.: Paulist, 1978.

Kelsey, Morton. *The Other Side of Silence.* Ramsey, N.J.: Paulist, 1976. The theory and practice of how we can be open to an experience of God.

Kelsey, Morton. *Companions on the Inner Way.* New York: Crossroad, 1983. Suggestions as to how to lead others to valid religious experience.

Kelsey, Morton. *Adventure Inward.* Minneapolis: Augsburg, 1980. Suggestions on the use of a personal journal to facilitate the experience of God.

Kelsey, Morton. *Afterlife.* New York: Crossroad, 1982. An understanding of the experience of the deceased in Christian history and experience with suggestions as to the nature of Christian afterlife.

Discernment of Spirits

Kelsey, Morton. *Discernment: A Study in Ecstasy and Evil.* Ramsey, N.J.: Paulist, 1978.

Gifts of Knowledge and Wisdom

Kelsey, Morton. *The Christian and the Supernatural.* Minneapolis: Augsburg, 1976.

Prophecy, Tongue Speaking and Interpretations of Tongues

Kelsey, Morton. *Tongue Speaking: The History and Meaning of Charismatic Experience.* New York: Crossroad, 1981.

The Gifts of Caring, Love, and Pastoral Care

Kelsey, Morton. *Caring: How Can We Love One Another?* Ramsey, N.J.: Paulist, 1982. How we can allow God's love to flow through us and make us true followers of Christ.

Kelsey, Morton. *Prophetic Ministry: The Psychology and Spirituality of Pastoral Care,* New York: Crossroad, 1982.

E. An Overview of the Depth and Meaning
of the Christian Faith

1. Von Hügel provided one of the most sophisticated modern analyses of the nature, depth, and relevance of the Christian faith for modern people.

Von Hügel, Friedrich. *The Mystical Element of Religion as Studied in St. Catherine of Genoa and Her Friends.* 2 vols. Greenwood, S.C.: Attic Press, 1961.

Von Hügel, Friedrich. *Essays and Addresses on the Philosophy of Religion.* 2 vols. Greenwood, S.C.: Attic Press, 1974.

2. I have tried to provide an overview of the meaning of Christianity in four books.

Kelsey, Morton. *Myth, History and Faith.* Ramsey, N.J.: Paulist, 1974. The meaning and importance of myth as revelation.

Kelsey, Morton. *Transcend.* New York: Crossroad, 1981. A popular overview of the meaning of Christian life and experience.

Kelsey, Morton. *Companions on the Inner Way.* New York: Crossroad, 1982. The nature of mature Christianity and how we can achieve it.

Kelsey, Morton. *Resurrection: Release from Oppression.* Ramsey, N.J.: Paulist, 1985. Shows that the resurrection of Jesus is only meaningful in terms of the total cosmic Christian drama and then gives suggestions as to how we can enter into the fullness of resurrected life.

INDEX